BLOOD, SWEAT, TEARS
AND FEARS

BLOOD, SWEAT, TEARS AND FEARS

Andy Till and Martin King

HEADHUNTER BOOKS

CONTENTS

ACKNOWLEDGMENTS

I would like to thank all the important people who have come into my life in one way or another. Carol Brown, the love of my life and soul mate. My beautiful, lovely children, Luke, Carly and Jack; Anna Till and Nicholas, John and Carol Till, and Natalie, Paul, Matthew and Matty, Ray and Joan Till and Family, Peter Till, Paul and Pauline Till and boys, David and Brenda, Donna, Martin and Joan Till, Jennifer and Dave Miller, Adam, David, and Zoe, Miller, Tony and Angela Grey and Family, Dave Brown and Michelle, Tom Brown, my stepson and Sally, Jimmy, Kelly, Holly, and Jimmy Wyatt, Sarah Brown, and John Brown, Pat and Gene Wilson, Pat, Andy, and Martin Wilson, Tony, Maureen, Dawn and Jenny Puddle, John Puddle and Family, Billy Puddle and Family, Jimmy Puddle and Family, Joan and Wiggy Puddle, Del, Del and Betty and the Wyatt family, Tony alias (flash garden) Katie, Joe, Paul Davey, Sarah Chambers, Steve and Laura, Dannella, leo, mark, Sue and Steve and Marks mum, Brian Nicholes, Alby Hunt, Jimmy and Wally Stockins and all their lovely families, Joe Smith (Joe Bug) Arron Smith, Little John Smith, (6ft 10 inchs) Rocky Kelly, Trevor Smith, Serg Fame, James Cook, W. O. Wilson. Wally Swift jnr, Robert Mcracken, Steve 'The Viking' Foster, Dave Stanley, Jason Stanley, Brad Bowler, Paul Bennett, Barry 'pitball' Britnall, Derrick (Chick) Costin, sadly missed to this day, Darren,Paul, Fraze Nally, Jamie (Talking Rubbish) Louisa Dandelion Merdock, Kelly and Alfie,

Peter and Marje winter, Paul and Karen and Family, Steve, Chris and Sonia Winter, Sally Bloomfield, Kelly and Natalie two lovely girls and Dave and Lee and all the kids, Johnnie Bloomfield (R.I.P) a top, top man what more can I say: Harry Holland, John Holland, Stuart Gee, Ted 'The Hairdo' Worrel, Rusty, Alan Gadd, Rory, Emily and the kids, John Paul and Janet Town, Gary and Jackie, Howe and Family, Graham and Amanda Stevens and kids, Carl Baxter, Lee Veins, Baldy Lee, Tubbs (Steve Hickman) Ian Marnak, Mark Constable, Tony Chapman and Lee Chapman, Don and Doll Town, Ian Taite, Anthony and Coline and last but not least my favourite auntie Edna; If I have missed anyone out who knows they should be listed here, then I'm very sorry but I must have taken too many punches during my career. But the good thing is I've still kept my good looks and charm. Also thanks to Martin King for helping write this book and bringing a lot, of both unhappy and happy memories out of my head and onto these pages. I hope you enjoy reading this book and thanks for buying or stealing it.

Best Wishes Andy 'Stone Face ' Till.

ROUND

1

CRUEL TO BE UNKIND

I WAS born on the 22nd August 1963 at Perivale Hospital Wembley, over in North West London. I was the youngest of 9 children so me coming along made it 7 boys and 2 girls. My brother John was the eldest and then came my sister, Anna-Marie. After that came my twin brothers Peter and Paul, and then my sister Jennifer, then brothers David, Raymond and Michael and then me, Andrew Gerald Till. And we all lived together with mum and dad in a 4 bedroomed house on the Shadwell Drive Estate in Northolt, North West London. We lived right opposite the Civil Engineer Pub. The difference in age between me and my eldest brother John is 12 years. My dad was from Paddington in West London and had worked as a gravedigger but I only knew him to work at Heathrow Airport as a baggage handler for British Airways, a job he stayed at for 29 years. My mum was German and came from Essen. They married a year after the Second World War finished. Fuck knows how they met. He must have dug her up when he was a grave digger or he took her in when she was on the run with the rest of the Nazi SS! She might have even been a German spy, but I tell you what, she was one evil woman. As I got older I learnt from my brothers and sisters that as the family grew my mum would ship out two or three of her children to children's' homes telling the Social Services that she couldn't cope. Apparently the same happened when I came along. Those of my brothers and sisters that were packed off for a while remember them times fondly. They've told me it was a relief to get away and eat properly and get some tender loving care and live a normal family life.

As a small child the only people I remember coming into the house was dad's brothers, Stan and George, and his sister Edna. My mum's family never ever visited as they all lived in Germany but I remember going out there a couple of times with my mum to visit my German Nan. We flew out there on cheap flights with my dad's concessions from work. Before we'd moved into the house where Id grown up, the family and quite a few of the older kids had lived in a prefab, which as the name suggests, was a prefabricated house made cheaply where all the sections were made for quick assembly. A lot of these places sprung up just after the Second World War as short term housing, but in some parts of London you can still find them with people still living happily in them.

All us kids had to get on because if there were any arguments then my mum or dad would punish the lot of us. The punishment could range from being sent to bed to all being bent over, having our trousers pulled down and having my dad's belt buckle end wrapped across our bare arses. It was pure humiliation, total child abuse. I can't remember ever sitting on my mum or dad's lap and getting a cuddle or any affection. We never really had any toys but I do remember we were once given a toy train set to share amongst the lot of us. We were never taken out, I mean all of us, on a family outing. Most weekends the four youngest kids were made to go with mum to a fruit and veg shop up at Lady Margaret Road. We'd push an old pram up there and wheel it out to the back of the shop and load it up with all the bruised and rotting fruit which the owners were going to throw out. We'd then wheel the pram home and mum would cut out all the rotten and bruised bits out of the freebies and keep the rest for us to eat. She always had a bunch of grapes and bananas on the sideboard but we were never allowed to touch them. My brother Paul once got caught eating a couple of the grapes and he got a clout around the head from my dad who asked why he had taken them. "I was hungry dad" was Paul's reply. "Right," said Dad, "you're hungry?" and he took a half a loaf of mouldy, brown bread which had turned green and blue, from the bread bin, sat Paul down with a glass of water and made him sit and eat the lot. He watched him eat every mouthful. I was about eight at the time and had already lost count of the beatings I'd suffered, many for the smallest of things. Something trivial could spark my mum or dad into giving us children a beating. If one of us had been deemed to have done something wrong and the rest of us wouldn't grass the culprit up, then we all got a whacking. We were never allowed to run around and play like normal children.

For school we had to keep the same gear on for a week. The shirt, trousers, vest, socks, pants and the home-made, knitted jumper was washed and ironed at the end of the week and put back on again on the Monday morning for school. It didn't matter how dirty it got or what was spilt down it, there was no change of school uniform and the jumpers mum knitted for us were like wire wool. If you scratched yourself down the face with it you'd be scarred for life. The jumpers were so itchy and uncomfortable but you dare not complain. As son as we got home from school we were made to change into a pair of shorts and a tee shirt or a sloppy Joe, as mum would call them. These also had to last us a week without a change. We wore black, slip-on plimsoles. Our school uniforms were then washed on a Saturday morning and we would wear it for church on the Sunday morning with a different colour tie to the one we wore for school. We were then marched off to church single file, with no talking, with dad at the head and mum bringing up the rear.

After school none of us would be allowed out to play with the other kids in our street. We had a telly and sometimes we were allowed to watch it for half an hour or so, but if there was horse racing on then we didn't get a look in because both mum and dad loved a bet on the gee gees. My mum's favourite punt was a 10 pence each way bet.

Every morning before us kids were sent off to school mum would stand at the front door and give us a tablespoon sized dose of sour milk. She claimed it was the same as yoghurt. Every now and again she'd replace the sour milk with a spoonful of cod liver oil. "It's good for you," she would say as she taunted us. She held our noses and forced it down our throats and that was the breakfast we ate before we set off on the 10 minute walk to school. At lunch time we'd walk back home for something to eat and every day it was the same. A boiled egg and a slice of dry bread, but before we could sit and eat it we had to run up to the betting shop with an envelope with my mum's bets for the day inside, and hand it over to the man behind the counter. As soon as we'd finished our lunch we would walk back to school. After school we were timed as to what time we got back. Mum knew what time school finished and how long it took to walk back. If we were as much as a minute late then it was another beating. Us kids did all the housework, hovering and polishing and tidying up while mum watched the racing to see how her bets were getting on. Sometimes dad would be home as he did shift work, but he never lifted a finger indoors.

Saturday was a slight change in the regime. We'd go to the church school in the morning and then be back at home about midday where either mum or dad would cook us a fry up. We'd get egg, bacon, sausage, mushrooms, tomatoes and baked beans and a slice of bread the size of a doorstep. We'd have that every Saturday and we weren't allowed to leave anything on the plate. This was all washed down with tap water as there was no such thing as fizzy drinks like coke or lemonade. They were unheard of in our house. Weekends were the only time us kids never went hungry. Our evening meal on school days was a slice of Edam cheese, one piece of bread and butter, and if the fruit wagon had rolled into town we might be lucky and get a piece of bruised or half rotten fruit. My eldest brother John and my sister Anna were now working full time and I can remember him bringing us younger ones home a bag of mixed sweets, and what a treat that was. I also remember John taking a few of us to London Zoo once, and that was a real treat.

Mum and dad never took us out on outings or days out. A Sunday morning at church was the highlight of our lives but what hypocrites my parents were. The church preached love and kindness to all and there these two were beating and starving their children, drinking, smoking and gambling. So where did religion come into it?

On Saturday, after the fry up, we had our weekly bath, and I mean our weekly bath. I was the youngest so I had to go last but the water didn't get changed and the bath washed out before the next one got in. Oh no, we were all made to bathe in the same water so me being the youngest had to sit in the grime left behind by eight other kids. There was no shampoo or nice salts to bathe in and all we had was a big lump of hard white soap which had no smell to it. Before I got in I'd cream the top layers of grime off the water with a plastic jug, and then pour it down the sink. Bath times was disgusting. I was in and out in a flash and would slip on the sloppy Joe and shorts, pants and socks I'd had on all week.

It was around this time that the smell of a roast being done in the oven would waft up the stairs. Mum would cook the Sunday dinner on a Saturday afternoon while she sat in front of the telly watching the horse racing and every week it was the same, roast pork with carrots, cauliflower, sprouts and roast potatoes. The meat was then re-heated in the oven on the Sunday and the cold vegetables covered in hot gravy to warm them up. It was unbelievable. One thing you should never do, and even I know this, is to re-heat cooked meat, especially pork. Fucking hell that's fatal. We could have ended up with food poisoning or salmonella or e-coli, but I suppose our little stomachs were used to it. The acid in our inners must have been like battery acid and digested and broke up any alien particles with the slightest resemblance to food. I shudder when I look back at times like that and as I say, at meal times we weren't allowed to leave a scrap of food. Nothing was left on any of our plates and if we had dared to ask for anything different to eat then we would have all got a slap. "Get on with it," my parents would have shouted accompanied with a back hander from dad around the head, or we'd get hit with, one of mum's favourite weapons of correction, a metal stair rod which was normally used to hold the stair carpet in place. But she had great joy in using it to hit us with. If we dare cry while the beatings were going on we'd get it even more. None of the others would try to defend you or say a word because whoever said a thing or tried to reason with them would be the next victim.

Most evenings after school, even in the summer months when it didn't get dark until around 10, we would have to be in bed by 6.30 p.m. at the latest. I remember the curtains were pulled and us kids would all in bed, even if it was a warm sunny evening and even though it could be hot and sticky inside we wasn't allowed to have the bedroom windows open. Through a crack in the drawn, well worn curtains you could at times see the sun still high in the sky and shining a ray of light into the room. I could hear the kids outside screaming and shrieking with laughter as they played hide and seek, and the sound of a ball being kicked up against a brick wall and bouncing back to the kicker, as squeals filled in the quietness as the seeker sought those hiding. I got up from my creaky bed still hungry and unable to sleep. I pulled back the curtains slightly and looked out. I just wished I could have been out there with all those kids. One of my brothers saw me and scrambled out of bed and knelt beside me. The next thing I felt a hand around my head as it sent me crashing to the floor, and a second later my brother landed on top of me. We hadn't heard dad creeping up the stairs to catch us watching normal kids outside just doing normal things like playing and having fun. He decked me first with a crashing back hander and then caught my brother with the follow up. Me and Michael, who I shared a bed with, were always getting caught for looking out of the window. One night, me and him were dragged out of bed and were hit across the bare legs with my dad's leather belt because he said he'd heard us looking out of the window. Some nights he'd send us off to bed and then wait outside the bedroom door and as soon as he heard a noise or suspected us of something or other then he'd burst in and sort us out.

Most nights it would be dad looking after us. Mum done a little office cleaning job and then after work without fail she'd go off to bingo. I don't ever remember her getting dolled up to go out. We had our weekly bath but on the whole her and the old man would bath at the most, once a month. They were dirty people and to this day I can still remember the smell they had about them. It was a musky B.O. sort of smell. When mum was at bingo and if dad had had a win on the horses, he might take us kids up to the local shop. He'd make us wait outside and he'd buy a couple of cans of pale ale or Worthington E, for himself. Normally he wouldn't buy us any sweets or comics or drinks but once or twice he'd buy one bag of crisps for us to share as we walked back home. Three or four pairs of hands would dive into a packet of Golden Wonder. The only time mum and dad went out together was to go to church but they thought the Till family were a respected family and were bringing their children up the right way. Mum was one lazy cow. If the thin blankets we had on our beds became threadbare she'd sew a patch on them. She even sewed the bottom sheet to the mattress so that she didn't have to wash it.

As I got older I was allowed a little bit more freedom and sometimes I would go to school friends' houses for tea and they'd sit and watch in amazement at just how much I could eat. I then realized that the way me and my brothers and sisters were being raised was not normal. Before I knew no better. My parents were not normal; they were evil, lazy, dirty bastards. They starved us kids and many a night I'd lay in bed hungry. One of my black mates from school used to have me around after school and his mum used to feed me up with her home made curried goat and chicken and rice, and years later when I told him what I'd been through he was shocked and told me that if his mum and dad had of known, what was going they would have taken me in and adopted me. I never told anyone at school what I was going through and to be honest I thought all families were the same as mine. Nothing was ever said, no social workers called in, and never any inquests about marks and bruises on my body from my teachers.

When I was about 10 mum took me out with a couple of the others to see my Nan in Germany. I remember my Nan cuddling me and me cuddling her. Mum clouted me around the head and pulled me off of her lap telling me to leave her alone as she was far too busy to be messing with me. Grandma said something to my mum in German and my mum looked embarrassed. When mum wanted to tell my dad something she didn't want us to know, she'd speak in German and my dad would reply in German. Us kids didn't have a clue what they were on about. Sometimes she'd shout at us in German and ruck and row with the old man in German. This was normally the time he rounded us up and took us off for a long walk. It was mostly on a Saturday evening when she'd lost on the horses and she was cooking next day's dinner. We'd walk about 2 or 3 miles to my dad's sister's house and back again. As soon as we got there auntie would get the biscuit tin out and offer us a biscuit. We'd look inside and see all them custard creams and chocolate digestives and shortbreads and ginger nuts and our mouths would be watering. Without even the walk we'd be hungry but we'd sadly have to decline auntie's offer because we knew if we took as much as a single biscuit we'd be in big bother when we got outside. Dad's sister was totally different from him, a clean and tidy woman with well brought up children of her own. Years later when we told her what we had been through she was shocked and said if she had of known she would have put a stop to it and done something about it. Auntie Edna is a lovely woman. Dad only went around to see her to get money off of her because he'd done his wages on the dogs or horses.

Another walk we'd sometimes get taken on was from our house along the canal path to Horsingdon Hill, near Sudbury Hill, which was fucking miles. The old man was in the army years before and he'd take us on this march that seemed to go on for hours. Our little legs struggled to keep up with him as he strode out with a left, right, left, right, arms swinging by his side. Once at the top of Horsingdon Hill we were allowed to go wild for half an hour and let off a bit of steam, and for that short time we were normal kids. He'd sit there oblivious to us, as he sat staring into space. Then he'd shout that it was time to go and off we'd march. Those that slacked off and didn't keep up with the pace would receive a clump around the head. We had Rex the dog but he never came with us. If it was a cold day we'd get home and Rex would be curled up in front of the gas fire. A swift kick up his arse would move him a bit sharpish as the old man would pull his chair nearer the flames and shout out one of our names to make him a cup of tea. Rex had his fair share of beatings too. He was a lovely dog but we wasn't allowed to play with him. It would be left to one of my older brothers to walk him and if he pissed or shit in the house because he hadn't been out for days, then poor old Rex would get it and so would all of us. He used to look at us with his big brown eyes, no doubt hungry like the rest of us. There'd sometimes be all eleven of us plus Rex and our cat in the tiny front room watching telly. Mum and dad would be smoking like chimneys and the heat from the fire and the smoke from the fags would almost choke you. No one was allowed to talk or move. If you got up to go to the toilet you were told to sit down. "If you go to the toilet pull the chain and wipe the seat," the old man would bark, not taking his eyes off of the flickering black and white screen. Once you'd been to the toilet you had to come straight back into the room and sit back down. He'd listen for your footsteps to hear if you'd gone upstairs or out into the kitchen.

In the summer we were allowed to play in the back garden for an hour after school. If any kids down the street knocked for you, you were allowed to speak to them at the front door. They weren't allowed in the house and you weren't allowed out. 5.30 p.m. we all sat and had our Edam cheese and a slice of bread and then we all had to wash our hands and face in cold water and then it was bed time.

Most of our clothes came from local jumble sales and hand-me-downs from my brothers. Everything was nylon. Nylon pants, nylon socks, nylon vests, nylon shirts. Someone else had worn everything, before.

Birthdays would be no different to any other day. There'd be no parties, no presents, and no cards up on the mantelpiece, no cake, no special meal. It was just a normal run of the mill day. Christmas was the same but we would have the traditional turkey dinner, but there'd be no cards or presents, no leaving a glass of milk and a plate of biscuits for Santa and his reindeer. If milk and biscuits had have been left out there'd have been a fight amongst us lot to see who got to the treats first. Our Christmas present consisted of an apple, an orange and a pear wrapped up in a brown paper bag. We sat down all together and the old man would say a few words and a sort of prayer before we was allowed to tuck in. Elbows were not allowed on the table and our wrists should be no further than two inches between the edge of the table and our plates. If our arms strayed further than permitted we would get mum or dad's knuckles wrapped on top of our heads.

Mum had a unique way of getting us kids up in the morning. She would come in, and grab our hair where we had a bit of side burns or use her knuckles on the soft part of our skulls. "Get up and make me a cup of tea," she'd growl in her sinister German accent. If she was in a good mood she'd just pull back the one itchy, woolly blanket the three of us in the bed shared, and throw a cup of cold water over us. One of us would have to go and make her a cup of tea and bring it up, and one of my other brothers would have to empty and wash out the plastic bucket she'd used to piss and shit in during the night. I couldn't begin to describe the smell. Sometimes the bucket would not be emptied for two or three days. It was hard not to throw up if you had the bad luck to be on bucket duty. Why not use the toilet?

In spite of all of this I don't think my school life was affected. I was quite a bright kid and loved sport. I enjoyed rugby but was banned from playing football for being too rough. As a few of my brothers and sisters got older, found work and moved out, they began to question the regime they'd been through and the way us four or five younger ones, who were still at home, were being treated. They'd get the same aggressive response which was "they're our kids and we treat them how we want and if you don't like it then get out." All the children had been through it but if you talk to my brothers and sisters they'll tell you that because I was the youngest I was spoilt. Fucking spoilt? I was beaten, abused and starved like the rest. Perhaps I may have got a more juicy orange one Christmas but that's hardly being spoilt is it? Through not eating properly and not having a balanced diet all us kids always had colds and cold sores around our mouths. We always had the sniffles and snotty noses but my brother David was about to change my life

ANNA TILL

I'm Andy's sister and I'm 14 year older than him, growing up with all them brothers and a sister, was lovely. It was a very strict up bringing and we all had our little jobs to do. It was tough there were 9 kids and only my Dad working, it was rough and tough for all of us. We had second hand goods and at times we had to go without, my God at times it was really tough. As I've grown up I've been more aware on how I was treated by my parents and I've bought my son up differently to how I was treated and I've tried to give him everything I never had, and I think Andy's done the same with his children. Nowadays kids seem to have much in the way of computers and machinery and they don't seem to be using their brains, and getting out and playing outside in the fresh air. When I was a kid we were never allowed out so we had to sneak out through one of the bedroom windows. I used to get walloped and beat black and blue by my Dad for no reason at all, he's broken my ribs and knocked me out with a punch and these things have scarred my life. Once Andy and one of my other brothers had to pull him off of me as he smashed me all around the house, again for no reason other then he was in a bad mood. I thought he was going to actually going to kill me. Mum would some times say something to try and calm him down but he'd tell her to keep her nose out of it, as he was the man of the house. My Mum was under his strict regime as well. My Mum was ill before she died and Dad was also ill but that didn't stop him from trying to rape her. I told him if you ever touched her again, then I'll have you and I told Mum to report him to the police, his reply was "they can't do anything she's my wife. He was one evil man. Before he died I didn't have a lot to do with him, I used to take their grandchildren around to see them, but the kids never liked going around there. I've told my children half about what went on, but kids nowadays are so much more street wise and it just would not happen without someone spotting it and seeing the tell tale signs. Andy didn't get on very well with my Mum and he'd blame her for a lot of things that went on, me and Andy were different to the rest and we'd speak our minds and they didn't like that. I used to stand up for myself against the brutality and I suppose that's what saved me from being killed. I used to go to most of Andy's fights, both pro and amateur and I'm very very proud of him, My dad went once and that was because Andy bought him the ticket but my Mum never watched him. He may act the big hard man but deep down he's a lovely bloke he's got a big heart, and he's got a heart of gold and he's always been there for me when I've had trouble in my private life. We've always kept in touch where as the rest of the family have all gone in different directions. A few of them have their own little cliques and to be honest I think they were always jealous of the relationship Andy and me have. Deep down I think in their own funny way they've proud of Andy but they'd never say it. I now live in Croydon, which is about an hour away from Andy. But we see one another as often as we can and we, speak regularly on the phone.

JOHN TILL

I'm the eldest of all the Till children where there was 7 boys and two girls. I'm now 55 years old. And I remember it was hard because there was that many kids in the house, clothes and other gear were a bit in short supply at times. Andy being the youngest had it a little easier as he didn't seem to have as many-hand me downs as the rest of us. My parents were very strict and the old man was never afraid to lay the law down. We were taken to church every weekend because Mum was German and was bought up as catholic so we were made to attend church, and go to Sunday school. Later on we were allowed to make up our own minds if we went to church or not. I suppose the rest of my brothers and sisters sort of looked up to me because I was the eldest and I was there for them if they had a bit of a Barney with Mum or Dad, I was a sort of peace keeper. I boxed at school and went to the local boxing club, me, my other brother David and Andrew all boxed, but I got into motor bikes and other things were as Andrew carried on. I followed Andy's career and I must have seen about 85% of his fights. I was well proud of him and what he's achieved where as if I'm honest some of the others in the family haven't stayed that close to Andrew but I suspect deep down if they were honest they'd admit to being proud of him. As we've all got older we've tended to grow apart, much the same as any other family, really. As a kid Andrew was no different to anyone else of his age he didn't really stand out as a tough kid or a little hard nut, but once he took up boxing his confidence and strength just grew. He's never been the easiest person to get on with and can be stubborn at times. Only the other day I was thinking back to when my daughter was a child and I'd take her to Mums and Dads house and she'd play with Andrew in the back garden, How time fly's?

ROUND

SECONDS OUT

MY BROTHER David, who is 6 years older than me, had taken up boxing at a local club. I was just over 11 and was full of energy and was intrigued by his tales of training at the gym. I kept asking him to take me with him but he would have none of it. I kept on and on. "The old man won't like it," he'd reply. But I still kept on and drove him mad.

One night the old man was on late shift and the old girl was at bingo so he relented and took me with him. The gym he went to was up near Northolt clock tower, which was a good 20-minute walk each way. An old boy called Billy Stag ran the club and I was so excited as me and Dave made our way up there. I jogged alongside him, my little legs struggling to keep up with him. I asked him a hundred and one questions to which he answered to all of them "just wait and see." We walked in and there was a few heavy punch bags hanging up and four posts with a rope between them for a ring. I had me playing out gear on with a pair of black plimsoles on my feet. David had been coming boxing for 6 months so he had all his gear in a bag. He'd had a couple of fights and was doing well. A few lads started shadow boxing and a couple went to work on the heavy bags hanging from the ceiling, and a few began skipping. I was told to shadow box and a few kids looked at the way I was dressed. I felt a right fucking idiot but I soon overcame the looks and stares and settled down to enjoy it, but the nice thing was at the end of the session I got to have a shower. Fucking hell! I was so excited. I'd never had a shower before. I stripped off and got straight under the jets of water. It was freezing cold but that didn't bother me. It felt good and I felt clean. The water washing over me was mine. It hadn't been over someone else before it got to me. It was virgin water. It was my water, my shower. I scrubbed and scrubbed and scrubbed. Fucking hell, this felt amazing.

That first night I hadn't even taken along a towel. I first used the tee shirt I'd worn for the training and when my brother was finished drying I used his towel. In the 12 years I trained at Northolt the showers never worked properly. They were either freezing cold or baking hot but from that first night I was hooked on boxing. I talked David into taking me a couple of nights a week when the old girl and the old man were out at bingo and working, and after a while everything began coming together and my skill levels and fitness improved.

I was now at senior school and encountered my first spot of bullying, which lasted all of 25 seconds. Some boy in the 5th year grabbed my home made knitted scarf, which my mum had made us kids knit ourselves, and lifted me up by it so that I was standing on my tip toes. He screwed the scarf tightly around my throat with his fist and pulled me towards him and we went eyeball to eyeball. As he happened to be doing this my brother Ray happened to be passing and stuck his nut straight on this kid's nose, and sparked him straight out. There was blood everywhere as Ray carried on walking with a smile on his face. He could have a tear-up, me brother Ray, but he was no bully. I straightened me scarf and carried on with whatever I was doing. So that was the end of me being bullied at school.

Although I was a fit kid and was doing well with the noble art I wasn't a confident kid. I was very shy. I'd been training about 3 weeks when mum and dad learnt that I was going boxing and after about 10 months I had my first amateur bout. I'd made a lot of friends down at the gym, among them the three Joseph brothers,

Chrissy, Mark and Matthew. They are lovely people and I still see them to this day. Also, one of the trainers, Pat Wilson's three sons, Martin, Patrick and Andrew were all good friends. Mark Griffiths, Ricky Redline, Brian Smith, and Brian Nichols who, like me, went on to turn pro, were good mates. Brian had about 10 fights and won eight. He later lost his licence and got banned for nutting his opponent and hitting the ref. We'd have a lot of travelling kids come and train for a while and then disappear, but overall it was a good crowd of fellas.

As I got to take the sport more seriously I needed some proper gear, like my own gum shield and a skipping rope and a sports bag to carry my gear in. I was sick of turning up at the gym with my moth-eaten towel in a plastic supermarket carrier bag. I asked mum for some money. "If you want money then go and get yourself a job," she'd growl, so that's what I did. I got myself a paper round and I got myself up and out of the house before the old girl came in and gave me a clump. It was a joy to be out of the house at 5.00 in the morning. No more piss pots for me. The only thing was I'd have to hand over a percentage of my earnings to the old girl and the rest I'd put away and save up for more bits of boxing gear. Also, my brothers Peter and Paul were now out working and they'd give me 50p a week which I'd tuck away and save towards my boxing. Them two were good to me and my brother Peter even bought me my first pair of boxing boots. They cost six pounds which at the time was a lot of money.

Almost from the first night at the gym my determination and strength could be seen. I was a very strong kid who wouldn't back down from anyone. I only knew one way how to box and that was to go forward. I made quality boxers cry and was constantly being told by the trainers to calm down and take it easy. My strategy was simple. Do them before they do me, and it seemed to work.

The paper round wasn't bringing in enough money and a mate of mine, Russell Smith, who I used to walk to school with, always seemed to have money, that much in fact he'd share his black jacks and fruit salad sweets with me. We had a lot in common because he'd had a hard upbringing, but he'd managed to get himself a job on a fruit and veg stall in Greenford. I asked him to ask the owner if there was any jobs going and it turns out the owner, Derek Costin, who everyone knew as Chick, was a mate of my boxing trainer Billy Stag, so I ended up getting a job there as a Saturday boy and fuck me, was I rushed off my feet? I used to get there at 6 in the morning and I never stopped. I had the job as a topper upper, which meant that if we were short of apples or pears or anything it was my job to keep topping up whatever we were running short of on show. I was like a blue arsed fly. Come 6.30 of a night when we closed and packed everything away, I was out on my feet. I knew I'd done a days work but the pay was good. Here I was, 12 years old, and I was getting five pounds a day, but then when I worked a couple of hours after school a few days a week., my money went up to ten pounds, plus I used to take home a big bag of fruit and veg plus all I could eat while I was there. The only downside was that mum got to keep all the gear I came home with and she'd take a third of my wages. But for the first time in my life I was eating properly, and healthily. I used to bring home the fruit and veg in a potato sack on the handlebars of me push bike and sometimes I might have ten to fifteen pounds worth of stuff. But the old girl never used to put it out for the rest of the family, but she'd do the same thing every week. She'd look inside the bag, wrap it all back up and take it upstairs to her bedroom and put it in the bottom of her wardrobe. Then once the gear from the week before had been used up she'd start using the stuff I'd bought home that week. Funny woman, a real hoarder who wasted nothing. I once looked in the bottom of her wardrobe and there was three sacks full of gear, so after a while I stopped bringing stuff home. The bike I used to ride backwards and forwards to work was one that me and my brothers had made up from scrap as kids, when we were allowed out, we'd go to the local rubbish dump and sort out old bikes and wheels and bring the bits back home and make ourselves up a bike. We'd take an old frame, stick some wheels we'd found on it, add brakes and tyres from another bike, put on a saddle and we'd have a custom-made bike made with our own hands and imagination.

My training at the gym was going well and I had a medical and got carded so now I could fight for my club. The first fight I had was over near Kew in West London. It was in a sort of scout's hall. I only knew one way to fight and that was to go forward. Billy's way of teaching you how to fight was double jab, right hand, double jab, but it worked for me at the time and I won my first bout. My prize was something I'd always wanted, a jigsaw puzzle! And if I remember rightly there was a bit missing, there was no medal or trophy, just a jigsaw puzzle! Still, it was a start. My trainer, Billy, had a fruit and veg stall in Southall Broadway and he used to meet up with Chick Costin at Great Western International Market where they'd both buy their gear. Chick was always asking Billy how I was doing and if I'd had any contests he'd ask Bill how I'd got on. Bill would say "yeah he won last week," and then back at the stall, Chick would ask me how I got on. I'd tell him the same as Bill had told him. "Good boy Andy," he'd say and give me a tenner on top of my wages. Chick was a lovely fella, someone I looked up to and trusted for the first time in my life. One thing's for sure, I didn't tell the old girl about my win bonus from Chick. I wasn't that silly. I used to hide my money under my mattress but a couple of times I had money go missing. I knew I could trust my brothers and sisters and it didn't take a lot of working out who'd taken it. I won more than I lost as an amateur but when I did lose I still told Chick the truth and he'd look me in the eyes and say, "good boy Andy, here's a tenner for not lying to me, Billy 'as already told me ya lost." He really was a lovely man. Years later when I won the Lonsdale belt I took it up to show him at one of his shops. "Andy I'm so proud of you," he said, and he hugged me and gave me a fifty pound note.

I left school at 15 with G.S.Es in English, Maths, and Geography and went full time on the stall. Things didn't change much at home and I still had to be in by 10 o'clock. If I wasn't I'd still get a clump around the head. Even though I was now 15 and physically strong and a good boxer I still wouldn't stand up to the old man. I was still frightened of him, both physically and mentally. As I got older my parents still never treated me with any respect.

When I was about 17 I started going to a local youth club and for the first time in my life I came across music and girls. At the youth club kids would bring in their records from home and play them on the old record player and they'd have it on full blast. My older brothers and sisters would sometimes have music on at home but mum and dad wouldn't let them have it on loud so I was never really brought up with music on in the house. You hear some people saying they were brought up with the sound of Elvis or Bob Dylan. I was never that lucky. I was brought up with the sound of pain.

One night a couple of the kids pointed me out to a girl called Jane telling her that I was the boy from the local newspaper who'd made the headlines about my boxing career. She was a pretty little thing and I was instantly interested. The local paper had recently run a story about me winning The Sportsman of the Month award, which was run by the Greenford Gazette. I went and collected the award at the Gillette Factory Social Club. Anyway, we got chatting and I took her out a couple of times to the pictures, and after a couple of weeks I took her home. As soon as we got in my dad started looking for a row and told me to do something or other and because I answered him back he back- handed me across the face. I was embarrassed. I looked at Jane and she'd gone as bright red as me. I went upstairs and the old man followed, still ranting and raving. I went into my bedroom and he came in and stood in front of me. I could hold back no longer and hit him with the perfect shot into his solar plexus, which if you don't know is the most vulnerable part of the stomach, just below the diaphragm. He dropped like a stone onto my bed gasping for breath. I moved in with clenched fists ready to finish him off. It was pay back time. I pulled back my arm and picked my spot as he lay there looking up at me, helpless. "This is for you, you bully cunt," I said to myself, and then I heard my brother Paul shouting "Andy no, you'll kill him." I stopped, looked at him, smirked and walked back downstairs. After 10 to 15 minutes my old man came back downstairs as if nothing had happened. "Come on we're going," I said to Jane, and we left. Outside she asked me what it was all about. "Nothing," I replied. "We're a funny family." She could see the red hand print the old man had put on my face but if it wasn't for my brother Paul shouting for me to stop and holding my arm back, I would have ironed the old man out once and for all.

ROCKY KELLY
BOXER

My respect for Andy came after the first time we met in the ring as amateurs. We'd both seen one another in the ring before and we had the utmost respect for each other even before we had the first of our three battles which were all close contests. For the record I won two of those bouts and he won the other but in truth they all could have gone either way. Andy was one of my toughest opponents. He was so strong and was as game as fuck. We're both more or less the same age but weight wise he's a bit heavier than me. I went on to fight Kirkland Lang for the British Welterweight title and Andy went on to win a Lonsdale Belt outright at Light Middleweight. We helped one another prepare for each others' fights and some of our sparring sessions in the gym were classics. We'd batter the fuck out of each other with people stopping what they were doing to watch us spar. They were hard sessions but that's the way Harry and John would train us.

I still meet Andy at functions or funerals and we chat about the old times. I don't really have a lot to do with boxing these days but I keep myself busy doing a bit of security with T.V. and film people, and I'm a glazier and painter.

ROUND

3

OUT WITH THE 1st
IN WITH THE 2nd

I ENDED UP seeing Jane for almost 18 months and that incident with my dad was never mentioned again. It was sort of serious with Jane and every so often I'd take her out to the pictures or meet up with her at the youth club. We also went out clothes shopping a couple of times and she tried to get me to splash out on the latest fashions, but I'd have none of it. There was no way I was paying out my hard-earned money on clobber and there was no way I was paying out fortunes for a jumper or jeans or on shoes. I was careful with me money. Who needs designer gear and why pay fortunes when you can get similar clothes for a third of the price?

I went on holiday with her and her mum and dad to Italy. She was half Italian. I remember I lost my virginity to her around her house when her mum and dad were out. I pulled one off before I got around there so that I'd make the dirty deed last longer and I'd impress her. The next day my cock was black and blue where I'd been banging away. I'd waited three months to shag her and it was worth the wait. It was her who instigated it and invited me around. She'd obviously done it before but I was a bit slow when it came to girls. Still, I had two minutes of fun with her. Her mum thought she was upper class and a bit of a poor snob. Her dad was Italian and in the end the mum and dad moved out to Italy to live. He got pissed one night and drove off the road and went over the side of a cliff and died. After that we just drifted apart but I did hear she got married and had a kid. Her mum and dad were always interested in my boxing career, more so than my own parents, and on the whole they weren't bad people. The mum used to say that boxing was a ruffian's sport. "Well, I am a ruffian", I would reply! And give her a wink and a cheeky smile.

Jane and me finally parted when she went on holiday to Malta with her sister. She met a local fella and romance blossomed, but it didn't last long. I wasn't too bothered because I'd met up with a girl I knew from school. Her name was Pauline and I was mates with her ex fiancé's brother, and he told me that they'd recently split up. She was a nice looking girl and to tell you the truth I'd always fancied her, along with most of the other boys in the school, but she'd never been that nice to me. If I'd tried to talk to her or tried to get her attention she'd tell me to "go away smelly," or "fuck off smelly". Her and lots of other girls would give me grief about my appearance. Anyway, I was a bit more confident now and a bit cleaner, so I gave her a bell and arranged to take her out. My social life and my boxing was on the up.

I'd fought Errol Christie in the Junior ABA finals and lost, but knew in my heart that I'd beaten him. I got to the finals three years running. One year, about two days before the final at some posh hotel in London, I was cycling to the gym and a car pulled out of a side road and knocked me off my bike. I went flying over the handlebars and hit my head on the kerb. Somehow I managed to get to the gym and stagger inside. The geezer that had knocked into me zoomed off and I was left with half me ear-hole hanging off. Billy Stag held my ear to the side of my head and let the blood congeal, which somehow held it in place. To pass my medical for the fight, Billy sprinkled my ear with flesh coloured talcum powder and it looked fine.

On the night of the fight my ear came undone with the first shot I took to the side of my head. This was the days before head guards came into the rules. When I fought Christie I wasn't nervous at all, I was scared of no one. In the first round I was roughing him up and in the second round I hurt him and he was hanging on. It was the classic boxer versus the brawler contest. He was the pretty boy boxer with great technique and I was the crash, bang, wallop boxer who only knew one way to fight, and that was to come forward throwing punches. He never hurt me once and he had no answer to me coming forward. I was just walking straight through his shots. When he got the decision I was disgusted and shook my head in disagreement. He never said a word to me after the fight, but we both knew I was robbed. At the time he was the golden boy of amateur boxing and an England International.

I also fought Chris Pyatt in the Junior ABA semi-finals. Chris later went on to fight for the World title and was a good pro. I also got into hot water when in a bout I kneed my opponent in the bollocks. I pleaded my innocence to the ref who gave me the benefit of the doubt, and after allowing the other bloke time to recover, the fight carried on. I won loads of trophies and cups but over the years they either got lost or me mum would sling them out. It could take up to six bouts to get through to the final and on one show I boxed three times in one evening. To get to the grand finals you have to win your area. Mine was the North West London ABAs. Many years later I met up with Chris Pyatt at an awards evening in London and we got chatting.

"What weight are you now Chris?" I asked him.

"Middleweight," he replied, "What weight are you Andy?"

"I'm Light Middleweight, but I'm thinking of moving up to Middleweight," I said.

"Well, let me know, because if you do I'll move up to Super Middleweight as there's no way I'd want to fight you again," he said.

Chris was a top geezer inside and outside the ring and I'd have loved to have got it on with him as a pro.

After about 10 amateur bouts I was matched up with Harry Lawson who at the time was meant to be the star of Repton, the famous East London boxing club. He was about 6'3" and was a big name on the circuit. They had great hopes for this boy but you know what? I beat him. I think I beat him comfortably. My style of fighting gave him big problems and I just mauled him for 3 rounds, which I won on points. I don't think he fancied it much. I fought him again in a re-match about 6 months later and beat him again over 3 rounds on points, and that was in the London Junior final. I remember I had a big, noisy support that night and the crowd really inspired me to do well.

Meanwhile, Pauline had matured into a good looking woman. She was from a working class background. Her dad ran a scrap yard and her mum worked in the canteen of a pharmaceutical company. I was driving by this time and I remember going around to pick her up in my rust coloured Austin 1100c.c. I thought I was very stylish and had past my test first time after having 30 to 40 lessons. I was still working at the fruit and veg stall and I suppose I was the apple of Pauline's eye. Pauline became interested in my boxing career and came to watch me in action in the ring. She kept me on the straight and narrow although I did have a bit of an altercation with a chap on a bus once, but that was before I met her and was still at school. I was on my way to work after school and was travelling on the 282 bus to Greenford. I was standing by the middle doors as the bus pulled up at my stop, and as the doors opened, a bloke came running down the stairs from the top deck and kicked me in the back. This sent flying off the bus and I end up lying on the pavement. I stood up and he came towards me. I hit him with a cluster of punches bang, bang, bang. My fists sunk into his face and he dropped to the floor. I grabbed hold of him and held his head under the back wheels of the bus, but before the bus can drive off and crush his head, two blokes in suits grab hold of me and pull me away from him. "You're nicked," says one. It turns out they're plain clothes coppers. Apparently the fella I'd just bashed up was 23 years of age and was known to the police as a bit of a tear away and a trouble maker. The thing was, as the coppers grabbed me I've clocked each of them with good shots. I bloodied one of their noses and put a mark on the others cheek. How was I to know they were Old Bill? I pleaded my innocence and told them I'd done nothing wrong and that the fella had come up behind me and kicked me off the bus. My claims fell on deaf ears and I was carted off to the police station. From there things seemed to go from bad to worse. The police didn't believe me when I told them my age and that I was still at school. I gave them my name and address and told them I was on my way from school to work at the stall, but because I was a big lad for my age and I had on a jean jacket instead of a school blazer they would have none of it. I was locked up in a cell for an hour and then they came in and asked me the same questions again about my age and where I was off to. I gave the same answers, which they didn't believe, and I was put back in the cells. This happened three times. Eventually one of my older brothers came down and got me out and we walked the three miles home from the police station. It was 8 o'clock at night and I'd been arrested at 3.40 in the afternoon. Dad was on late shift and mum was at bingo so they weren't home. In the end I went to court and received a 50 pound fine and was bound over for a year, which was a lot of money then. The bloke I'd hit was bound over and I didn't get charged for hitting the two coppers. It could have been a lot worse. Imagine if the bus had of run over the bloke's head? Imagine if the coppers hadn't of been there? At the time I was in such a temper but I'm glad no real harm came to anyone.

After about 8 months of seeing Pauline we got engaged. I was 19 and we had the engagement party at The Red Lion in Greenford. Because of the boxing I didn't really drink alcohol. Well, I say I didn't drink but if I went into a pub at 7 o'clock at night and got a pint I'd still have the same pint at 11 o'clock, and then it would only be a weak larger shandy. I wasn't really a boozer and neither did I ever smoke. From the age of 12 I had this dream of turning pro as a boxer, winning a Lonsdale Belt outright and then moving on to bigger things. About 150 people turned up at the party and we had a good night.

I always had to watch my weight though. I'd just boxed for England against Kenya and went on to box twice more for my country. I was proud to represent my country in the ring but had no real aspirations to box in the Olympics. I was setting my sights much higher.

At 20 Pauline and me tied the knot and got married. We'd been together 18 months and we had a big, white wedding but didn't go on honeymoon. We couldn't really afford it as we'd not long bought a flat down Lady Margaret Road. It was a two bedroomed flat, which I got off me Brother David. We paid about 34 grand for it. Her dad, who was now a painter and decorator, helped us do it up. I liked her mum and dad, they were good people. She also had two sisters, one lived down at Hastings and we didn't see a lot of her, and the other one was a stuck up cow who thought her shit didn't stink, and was a bit snooty. She won't like me saying that but that's how she came across. I knew her husband Mark as we went to the same school, and he's lovely fella. She aint a bad sort really, I've met worse.

After 18 months of marriage Pauline announces she's pregnant and we set out to find a bigger house. Just before she gives birth we move into a brand new Bovis home in Yeading. A few months later she had our first child and we call him Luke and he looks just like me. Well, all babies look like me with no hair, flat noses and squashed faces! I was there at the birth and I was as proud as punch.

I also left my job at the stall and became a milkman. Lots of things were changing in my life. I was now a family man with responsibilities but I needed to be bringing in more money what with the new house and the extra mouth to feed. There was only one way and that was to turn pro. After nearly a hundred amateur contests it was time to mix it with the big boys.

HARRY HOLLAND
BOXING MANAGER – PROMOTER

I knew Andy from when he was a kid and he was boxing for Northolt and I was at Hogarth Boxing Club. I first saw how he could be when he fought Rocky Kelly. They met 3 times in the ring as amateurs with Rocky winning twice, and believe me, they could both have a row. I've always had an interest in Andy and we've always got on well. I remember when they were about 15 years old and Rocky was getting some stick off of some other kids at a show and Andy clocked what was going on and shouted out "here Rocky I'll have some of that." Although they'd bashed one another to bits in the ring, outside it they were prepared to stand by one another. That says a lot about the pair of them. Pat Wilson, Andy's trainer, always kept me up to date on Andy's progress and when there was talk of him wanting to turn pro I invited him over to the pro gym I was then running, for a chat. He signed up with me, and he was a pleasure to train. Yeah, we used to have our rows but underneath that rough exterior there's a decent bloke.

One time I had 22 professional fighters on my books. Andy was one of my better fighters but I had James Cooke who won the British and European titles. He had the skill but didn't have Andy's guts and courage. I first took my pro licence out in 1982 and when I first started I had close links with Frank Warren who I must say helped me no end. I started with Gary Hobbs, Micky Harrison and Rocky Kelly. All my fighters were in the same league, all committed and all with bundles of courage. The worst thing to me Andy ever done was pack up his milk round. He was up early every morning and was fit with fresh air in his lungs as he scooted around delivering the milk. It was great for his boxing training, but then he went over the airport and it was a lazy job and he was drinking tea and eating biscuits. He stayed with me right through his pro career and we had lots of highs and a few lows and after the Robert McCracken fight I, in all honesty, thought it was time for him to call it a day. He then had an 18-month, lay off and came back down the gym and said he wanted to give it one more go. The trouble was he'd put on so much weight with what I call his lazy job. He'd lost the will to get fully fit and motivated, plus the boy

Darren Griffiths who he fought in his come back was no mug. He lost that fight and it really was time to call it a day. I know that in my heart, and with a bit of luck, he could have been a world champion. He really was that good. What he lacked in the skill factor he more than made up for in his courage, strength and heart. He had the heart of a lion. He would fight anyone put in front of him. I'll praise Andy to the hilt. Look at when he fought Laurent Boudouani. He was only beaten by Boudouani by a blatant head butt and Boudouani went on to win the world title, so Andy was right up there with the best. We paid Boudouani and his people a lot of money to come to London to fight.

Nowadays Andy would no doubt be a world champion. There was a time it was hard to match Andy with fighters because he had such a reputation for being a tough bastard. I was offered Chris Eubank as an opponent for Andy, in Eubank's early career that was. I spoke to Ronnie Davies, Chris's trainer, who I knew from the amateur days, and he told me that Eubank was a bit special, and he wasn't wrong. He went on to have a fantastic pro career and entertained millions of fight fans. It would have made for a great fight between them. It would have been a clash of the styles with Andy coming forward all guns blazing and Eubank picking him off and being patient. For all that's been said about Chris Eubank you can't take away the fact he was a very clever fighter. When Andy finally packed up I still had a few fighters left. I had Trevor Smith and Courtney Fry who was 3 times A.B.A. Champion and Commonwealth gold medalist, and Carlos Chase who were all good fighters. Slowly but surely the amateurs coming through into the pro ranks began to dry up so I decided to wind things up.

I even had Andy's ex wife come in the gym one day shouting her mouth off about how I should run my gym. I told her firmly but politely not to get involved in his or my boxing affairs. I asked her outright "do you go out in his milk float with him and tell him how to deliver milk?" She couldn't answer. I've had rows with my boxers but things have never really got out of hand. I've called them cunts and they've called me the same but we've never come to blows. I now do a bit of acting and have been in Eastenders for the last 19 years and have really enjoyed it.

Sadly I recently lost my long time friend and trainer, Johnnie Bloomfield, who was a great pal. Me and him worked together for years and we were a great double act. All the time we were in the corner together he never talked over me or butted in when I was talking to the boxers. He was a real joy to work with and we all miss him terribly. I now work as a cuts man and I've been diagnosed as having cancer which I've been fighting for the last 15 months. I recently worked in Audley Harrison's corner when he fought Danny Williams at London's XL Centre. Personally I don't like the state of pro boxing these days. There are boxers promoting themselves and training themselves. Give me an Andy Till any day.

ROUND

WHEN ANDY MET HARRY

FOR THE life of me I can't remember the events that led up to me turning pro but I did, and went with boxing promoter and manager Harry Holland. I was working as a milkman during the day and training at Harry's gym at Ealing Leisure Centre at Sudbury Hill three nights a week, and on a Sunday morning. I'd get there on training nights about 5.30 and train till about 10 o'clock. Johnnie Bloomfield was my trainer and good at it too. He was good at lifting you up and geeing you up. Harry had some good pros on his books and the first night I walked in there, there was Rocky Kelly who I'd fought as an amateur four times, winning once and losing the other three. There was also Gary Hobbs who was a great boxer whose career was cut short by a freak accident. He was so good that in my view he could have gone on to be British, European and even World champion at his weight. I must admit I was a bit nervous on my first night. I'd had a medical, got my licence to fight as a pro but by nature I'm a shy person so I was a bit apprehensive. I got a warm welcome from the boys though, as a lot of them knew me from my amateur days.

With the first night training under my belt I felt a lot better. I drove off home in my white Escort van feeling quite pleased with myself. I felt a million dollars as I pulled out of the car park and got admiring looks from some of the kids from St. Patrick's amateur gym who shared the same building as the pros. My Escort van was like no one else's. For a start it had windows cut into the side and it had a back seat in the rear that used to fold down almost into a bed. It was my love machine, my love truck. I used to think I was the bees' knees in that motor and in a way I suppose I was.

After a few weeks I got into the swing of things and I used to have some right ding dong battles with Rocky. When we were sparring we'd do sometimes 8, 10 and even 12 rounds, and 30 odd people would stop what they were doing and watch us. It was a proper row, a proper war, but at the end we'd always touch gloves and hug one another. We'd knock lumps out of each other but there was nothing but total respect between the two of us. I'd been training for around six months when Harry came into the gym one night and announced to us all that he was putting a show on at the Leisure Centre where we trained. He told me that I was on the bill and that I had 5 weeks to get myself ready, and that I would be fighting a Peter Reid who was also known as Peter Vance. For my sins my purse for the fight was 350 pounds. I knew nothing about my opponent, only that it would also be his first pro fight.

The night before the fight I had an early night and was up early and had me 3 shredded wheat. Then it was off for the medical and then the weigh-in. The medical was conducted by a doctor from the British Boxing Board of Control. He or she checks your eyes, ears, heart, blood pressure and all that. Your weight in a non-title fight is not as important as a Title fight. There's a little bit of leeway so the odd pound or two over is normally accepted. I'd personally sold nearly 200 tickets for the fight and it was a relatively small venue so I was guaranteed a good support. I got to the venue 3 hours before the first fight and walked around the place and took a look around. I then found a quiet corner in the changing rooms and had a kip for an hour or so. There'd be people buzzing around and looking for gloves and towels and bits and pieces, but I'd get a bit of shut eye. I had a few butterflies but I wouldn't say I was nervous.

Half an hour before the fight the ref came in and said his bit to me, I got my hands bandaged up and then got gloved up and started warming up. I just wanted to get out there and get it on and fight and get it over with. I just loved fighting. I'd do a bit of shadow boxing and get a bit of a sweat on. "Come on Andy let's get warmed up," my trainer Johnny Bloomfield's deep voice boomed out at me. He was a lovely man John, but sadly he's no longer with us. Harry was in and out like a blue-arsed fly and looked more nervous than me. Pauline, my wife, came in and gave me a kiss and wished me good luck.

I think I was third or fourth on the bill and I was anxious to get out there. Then it happens and we get the call to leave our dressing room. We made our way towards the ring, and as we walked into the arena the noise of the crowd hit me. It's like a rumbling sound, almost dream-like. I could hear people shouting and cheering and I could even see their mouths moving. Some had eyes bulging and some were smiling, but I couldn't make out what they were shouting. I walked up the steps on the outside of the ring and ducked between the ropes. John offered me a drink from a plastic bottle and I took a swig, spat it out and bounced up and down on the canvas. My opponent was across the other side of the ring and our eyes met and I never took my eyes off of him. If he had of looked away then I knew I was already halfway to having him beat. We came together in the middle of the ring and John's rubbing away on my shoulders as the ref gives us the instructions that he wants us to obey. My eyes are burning into my opponent's and it's game on. Let's get it on. We turn and go back to our corners, the bell goes and we come out fighting. The first round I come out too eager and come out all guns blazing. I'm fighting with a lot of my amateur ways and after the first round my corner tell me to slow down, keep it nice and tight and go steady. The thing was I didn't let him get into his rhythm and bullied him out of his stride. I couldn't wait to get out for the next round as I was enjoying myself. To me the bell just gets in the way of me having fun. Who needs to stop for drinks and a chat? It was a boxing match not a fucking dinner party and stopping in between rounds only spoilt the fight.

The next 4 rounds went the same with me doing all the pressing and landing the better shots. In the sixth and final round I caught him with a barrage of shots and the ref deemed he was unable to defend himself so stepped in and stopped the fight. I was on a real high and after that first fight I don't think I even stopped at the venue for a shower. I just towelled myself down and got changed. Pauline came in to check on me and so did a few of my brothers. Even the old man came to that fight only because I paid for his ticket. The tight bastard. I never offered again and he never came again. Mum never came. She must have been at bingo Or counting her winnings from the horses.

The next day I went up to the gym and collected my money off of Harry. 350 pounds wasn't a lot of money but Pauline was happy and my earnings were boosted when I copped 10 per cent of the tickets I'd sold for the fight.

Three weeks later I was back in the ring at Crystal Palace to fight Graham Jenner who'd had 7 fights, winning 5 and losing 2. He was the favourite to win but I was a fancied underdog. I'd been the underdog all my life and I loved proving people wrong. The fight went well and I beat Jenner on points over 6 rounds.

Next up was Randy Henderson on the 10th November 1986 at The Heathrow Park Hotel over near the airport. This fight made it 3 quick fights on the spin it was all happening so fast since making my pro debut in the September. Now I was up against Henderson, just over a fortnight since my last victory. Still, I didn't care as I'd have fought every day if I'd been allowed to. Henderson was one awkward fighter who had had 22 fights, winning 6, losing 15 and drawing one, but he had the ability to make you look ordinary. He was an awkward looking fucker with great big, long arms. It was the same old tale, smash 'em and bash 'em and take no prisoners, but I couldn't get past his long, muscley arms. Every time I teed him up to let a decent shot off he'd tie me up. His style was very hard to work out. He was a pain in the arse and although I had a frustrating night I still beat him on points.

In January 1987 nearly two weeks after Christmas, I was again back in action against Tony Lawrence at Ealing Leisure Centre. He'd only had a couple of fights and had lost both. He was a bit heavier than me and was a full-blown Middleweight. He was about 6'2" to 6'3" and was a big fucker. I was shorter than him and during the fight I'd duck under his jab and come up and land my shots. As I moved in he'd hold the back of my head down with his gloves and this must have happened a hundred times I moved in again and fired off some shots, again he held my head down and pulled me into his chest. This time I could feel my gum shield coming out of my mouth so I bit into it to stop it falling out, but in the action I must have dislodged my gum shield and bit him in the chest. It was an accident well that's what I told the ref. Anyway that stopped him holding me. As he let go off my head a bit sharpish he screamed, "Ref he's just bitten me." I stood up and grinned at him and looked at the ref but the ref just smiled back, waved his arms, "Box on" he instructed. When I got back to my corner I got an almighty bollocking from Harry. "What the fuck are you playing at?" he asked, shaking his head in disbelief. The fight lasted until the 4th round when the fella was out on his feet and the ref stepped in and stopped it.

About a month later I'm back in the ring against another full blown Middleweight, Ian Bayliss, who'd had 3 previous fights. He was a big strong, stocky looking fella. The West London Hotel in Fulham was packed to the rafters as Harry had put on a top class bill. My stable mate, Rocky Kelly, was fighting the legendary Kirkland Lang who later on in his career fought and beat Roberto Duran. Duran was my man. He was one of my all time favourite boxers. He had the lot, skill, speed, strength, courage and a sense of humour. He's a one off. When I got in the ring and looked at Bayliss he looked more like a Super Middleweight or even a light Heavyweight. I'd say he was a good stone and a half heavier than me but I'd come to fight and so had he so let's get it on.

The bell went and he caught me with a good shot, and fuck me did it hurt? I cracked him a good shot straight back and it hurt my hand. Fucking hell he had a head as hard as a coconut and my fists were just bouncing off of his nut. He never budged. As we came in close he grabbed me and rubbed his head in my face. As the ref told us to break and we moved away from each other, I could feel blood trickling down my face and then I knew he'd done me with his head. Blood was coming from above my right eye and this was the first time in my career that I've had a serious cut. I'd had the odd nick here and there but I could feel this was more serious. My corner done a great job and managed to patch me up and I ended up winning the bout on points over 6 rounds. Nothing was said after the fight about the excessive use of his head but then again I've never really had a lot to say to my opponents before, during or after a fight. I'm a man of not many words and I liked my fists to do the talking in the ring. As I said before, I'm quite a shy person and have never gone looking for trouble outside the ring.

Next up was Dean Scarfe who I was told had just come out of nick. He'd had eleven fights and won 9 and lost 2. He was from Wandsworth so the show was in his home town. He was a white south paw who again I'd say had a good weight advantage over me. He was tall as well, around 6'3' and with an attitude to match. He thought he was the dog's bollocks when he got into the ring. As we came together in the middle of the ring before the first bell and went eyeball to eyeball, he was glaring at me and I was giving him the evil eye back. The ref gave us his instructions for a nice clean fight and to obey the rules at all times, blah, blah, blah and I turned to walk away back to my corner. Just then, out of the corner of my eye I saw spit fly through the air and just miss me. The cunt had spat at me. I had the raving hump now, the dirty bastard. I know he deliberately spat at me to try and intimidate me. I lost that fight on points and I'm not making excuses but it was my first 8 rounder, I'd had two days notice to take the fight, he was heavier than me and we fought in his own back yard. As a pro you have to keep yourself half fit but his original opponent had dropped out and I was a late replacement. I still thought that I beat him. Still, I earned meself 500 pounds but I suffered my first taste of defeat as a pro. I look at it like this. On the 30th April 1987 at Wandsworth, it says on my boxing records that I lost to Dean Scarfe over 8 rounds but in my heart I know I won that fight. He never hurt me once but I roughed him up. The only injury I nearly incurred was when I nearly slipped up on the gob he spat at me in the ring.

I had about six months out of the ring after the Scarfe fight but I was back stronger, fitter and more determined. My next fight was against Andy Wright in the September at the Crystal Palace Sports Arena. I got an 800 pounds purse for that fight, nearly doubling my money from when I first started as a pro. At that time Andy Wright was being touted as a future golden boy of British boxing. He was a roofer from South London, all toned up and permo-tanned with a body builder's physique, what you might call nowadays a Chav. Out of the ring he'd probably be all blinged up with a snide Burberry baseball cap and no shirt on. You know the type, you see them up the downs Derby day or at Kempton market. He had a record of 7 fights, winning 5, losing 1 and drawing 1, but give him his due he could bang and he could box a bit as well. He had knocked a lot of his previous opponents out. He had a similar style to me, he knew if he hit you right you'd go. Andy Wright could take you out with either hand so I had to keep my guard high and get my own shots off before he teed off. I had a plan, and that was to take the centre of the ring and back him up from there.

In the first round he caught me with some good decent shots. They were that good it was like a camera flash in front of my eyes and a split second later my head would clear and I'd recover and hit him back with some good shots of my own. The first round I'd say was evens. In the second round I caught him with a body shot and then a right hand over the top. That was it. He fell to the canvas. The referee took up the count and he got to his feet but his legs were like rubber. The ref had no choice but to stop the fight.

It's February 1988 before my next bout and I'm up against Geoff

Sharp at The Crest Hotel, Longford. He had a record of 4 fights, 4 straight wins. He was another full blown Middleweight who could bang and was very durable. In the fight I done me usual, all over my opponent like a rash but he just moved away and jabbed. In the second round he hit me with a shot that nearly took my head off. It felt like my head had spun right around full circle like the girl in 'The Exorcist.' Film. It spun back around again and I remember looking up from the canvas thinking "oh fuck, I'm down, I'd better get up." I was down on my arse. When I look back at that fight on video you can see and hear the shot. It sounds like a leather cricket ball hitting a wooden bat, the sound of leather on willow, I think the saying is? I walked straight onto it as he threw it. When I got back to the corner my trainer, John, asked if I'd seen the punch coming. "If I had of done John I'd have got out of the way," I replied. I still can't believe how I got up from that shot. It took a good 4 or 5 seconds for my head to clear and for me to realize where I was. As I got back to my feet the ref asked me if I was alright to carry on and I nodded and replied "yes," and held my gloves up to my head to indicate that I was alright to continue. "Box on," barked the ref and Sharp came steaming into me. He must have hit me with 40 to 50 shots in 20 seconds but I clung on in there. The bell went to end the round and I wobbled my way back to my corner on rubber legs that didn't seem to belong to me and legs that I had minimal control of. I was like a new born giraffe. My corner tipped water over me and worked away fanning a towel in my face. My head still hadn't cleared by the time we came out for the third round and then straight away he caught me again with a peach of a left hook, which knocked me across the ring. The crowd was going wild. He had a big gypsy following and they were cheering their man on to finish me off. Some how I found my composure and got back to work picking him off with solid jabs. I could see both his eyes were badly swollen and I started to get on top as his eyes were beginning to close. At the end of the third John leant through the ropes as I sat on the stool. "Andy, don't get caught with another one of them shots," he said. I looked at him with disbelief. Did he really think I was meaning to get hit with good shots? Words of wisdom from John that I really didn't need to hear.

In the fourth I came out and was picking him off. I'd gone up a gear and my speed and power had turned the fight. He'd hurt me and I'd refused to give in and that definitely disheartened him. His bottle started to go as the snap went from his punches. I hit him with a good combination of punches and he went down on one knee. The ref took up the count and he was up on his feet at 8 or 9 but the ref had seen enough and stopped the fight.

After nearly 10 months out of the ring I was back in the November for a 10 rounder against W.O. Wilson and I'd even surprised myself by going out and doing some road work. I'd never been one for getting up at 4 in the morning and pounding the cold, dark streets, but I guessed for this fight I'd have to as this was my first 10 rounder. W.O. stood for Winston Oliver and he was a big fella who was also a male model who had a lot of female support. He'd had 9 fights and won 7, losing 2. He was another south paw who'd beaten Jimmy Cable as a pro so I knew he'd be more than a half decent fighter. He was a handsome black fella and a nice geezer with it.

The fight was at Battersea Leisure Centre in London and the place was packed. The fight was very close in the early rounds and then I started catching him with some good shots and in the 5th and 6th I had him wobbling. He went down on one knee but he claimed to the ref not to take up a count because he'd slipped. The ref listened to him because as soon as he got to his feet there was no count and a "box on". Later on in the fight Mr. Wilson must have got a bit peckish because he took an almighty chomp on my ear. Again the ref saw nothing wrong, told me to shut up and to box on. Yeah right, like the slip. I caught him then with a perfect right hand left hook combination that put him down. Around about the 8th round I really had to dig in deep to keep going. I'd done 6 and 8 two minute rounds and I'd also done 8 x 3 minute rounds but this was

10 x 3 minute rounds and my chest felt like it was going to explode at times. It was very hard. Anyone who says they can box 10 rounds comfortably is a fucking liar. The way I fought I was always marching forward, being aggressive and using up plenty of energy. Before the end of the fight I managed to get in close to him and I bit his left cheek. The ref shouted, "stop boxing," and pulled us in close to him. "Right, you've both had a bite and a taste of each other so now let's have a clean fight." "Box on." Straight away Wilson threw a right hand and I came up with a left hook and a right hand and an elbow into his stomach. It was more in keeping with wrestling than boxing but Mick McManus would have been proud of me as Wilson reeled back from my almost perfect forearm smash. "Sorry ref," I said, struggling to stop my gum shield from coming out my mouth as I pissed myself laughing in fits of giggles. The ref could even see the funny side to it as he smiled and ordered us "box on." I won the contest on points but it was a tough, tough fight. In the first round I'd fractured my middle knuckle and Johnnie Bloomfield had to push and pull it back into place but fucking hell, did it hurt? I put it in an ice bucket and it came up like a balloon.

After the fight I felt like I'd been run over by a train and then the train had come back and reversed over me ten times. I ached all over. I got home around midnight and ran myself a hot, steaming bath and poured in some Radox bath salts and laid in it until 7 o'clock the following morning. As the water got cold I'd let some out down the plug hole and top it up with more hot. I then went to bed and didn't get up for a day and a half. I was fucked. Harry came around to see how I was and was on the phone to me every few hours. It was worse than a bout of triple flu. I'd put everything into that fight but I take my hat off to Winston Wilson. He was a great opponent and we've remained firm friends ever since. A few years later I even helped him out of an embarrassing situation but I'll come to that a bit later.

PAT WILSON
AMATEUR BOXING TRAINER

I've been at Northolt boxing club for 33 years now, and I first met Andy when he was aged 11. His elder brother David who at the time was about 15, use to box here and bought Andy along one Sunday morning I thought Andy had come straight from playing football because he had muddy knees but he told me he'd come straight from church. Then he told me later that he used to bunk off of going to church and go and play over the local park. Andy had the physique of a 14-year-old and was very strong for his age. At the time Billy Stag was the main trainer here and I was just helping out with him, and we had Andy doing bits and pieces with a bit of skipping and bag work but he was very keen. Even at that early age you could see his strength and aggression and we knew he was going to be a bit special, we even had trouble, finding boys to spar with him. Even my two boys, who were roughly the same age as him found him to strong for them, he just had that ability to take a punch. I remember his first bout over at Roehampton when he received a jigsaw puzzle for fighting, and if I remember rightly there was a piece missing. Afterwards the boys that had boxed were all given one sausage roll and a glass of orange squash each. In them days our gym fees were 10p each nowadays its £3 for seniors and £2 for the juniors. Andy went on to win the 'Area Schoolboys' and the regional A.B.As, but he lost in two junior ABA finals one to Errol Christie and one to former WBO middleweight champion, Chris Pyatt. He always seemed to come up against the same kid, in the schoolboys, and that kid was Rocky Kelly. Andy fought him 4 times and they were always close battles but good fights but if anything I would have given the decisions to Andy whom if I remember, only beat Rocky once. But as I say they were brilliant fights, they were all close but the fights were mostly on Rockys club shows so if there was any doubt on a winner then the judges might just favour the home boy. But they've always remained good mates. Harry Holland was a trainer we'd frequently bump into at shows and when Harry started up his own pro gym I just think it was a natural progression for Andy to sign up with him. They'd become sort of mates over the years.

Personally I would have liked him to have gone and trained with someone like Jimmy Tibbs and Terry Lawless who I think would have got a lot more out of him and with their connections, I'm sure would have taken him a lot further. The thing was Andy was working full time and Jimmy and Terry would have wanted him to train during the day time and do the evening sessions, plus there was the journey from North West London to the East-end, where as Harry's gym was an evening thing, and it was closer to home for Andy. I watched him all through his pro career and was well proud of him. As a kid he was rough and ready and a bit of an hand full but he was never cheeky. He was a bit stubborn at times but most of the time he was a real joy to be with. His kips or cat naps before fights were legendary. We were at one show and he was the sixth bout on the bill, so as fight number three's finished I've thought to myself I better start getting Andy ready for his fight, and I've looked everywhere but can't find him. I was ready to give up, and I was starting to panic a bit, when I saw a pair of boxing boots and the bottom of a corduroy dressing gown sticking out from a cupboard door under some stairs. I pushed open the half-closed door and there he was sound a asleep. He's still pretty much the same, well-laid back and I thought he would come back one time and help me at the club. I think he should put some thing back into boxing because he's got so much knowledge and experience to pass on it would be a shame to see all that go to waste. Before his big European fight I didn't realise just how bad his family life was. I always thought he ad a lovely little family and that everything was all right. But that night he got in the ring I knew some-thing wasn't right there was no fire in his eyes no aggression in his posture and his body language just wasn't right. I went to his dressing room after that fight and he'd been cut to pieces and I told him he should now call it a day. The next thing I heard he'd split up with his missus and had planned to fight again. He started to come down here to prepare for this fight, and sort of trained but you could see it wasn't the old Andy he was doing some bag work and he was puffing and panting and all he wanted to do was rabbit. He was over weight and unfit, but he wouldn't listen. He thought his strength would get him through but it didn't and the rest as they say is history. Over the years we've had some good boys down here turn pro, we've had, Brian Nichols, Anthony 'The Monk' Mcfadden who had 17 pro fights and won them all, he was light-middle and then moved up to middleweight, he was in the same camp as Howard Eastman. He was an Irish kid that didn't turn pro till late because he had a good job as a surveyor. His camp wanted him to give up his job and concentrate on a title fight, but he said no and turned his back on the fight game. We also had Mickey Lloyd who was a good fighter that had 16 fights and won 14. We've had Rodney Harrison who was really a basketball but trained here, his brother Audley who used to come along to watch originally but then took up the training and stayed here for four seasons. He travelled from Hackney in East London and some nights it would take him hours to get here, one night it took him 6 hours to get over here. Anyway he ended up boxing at the famous Repton club, which was only one bus stop away from where he lived. But when he won the ABAs he came back here and done all his sparring with my big heavyweight, William Bereamer. Later on William turned pro and won his first fight in the 1st round. In his 2nd fight he was put in with some big Norwegian champion and knocked him out, the thing was with William, was that he had a good dig and could punch. In his 3rd fight he was thrown in with someone for a wanky world title, and got beat as a last minute opponent, after some Russian pulled out. After that he only boxed one more time against Wayne Llewelynn, who was a good 3 to 4 stone heavy then Willie and then after that he called it a day. I've probably had half a dozen boxers here turn pro and all of them have done relatively well. But Andy was the special one and he meant a lot to me. Now and again he pops into see us and lots of the boys here look up to him and the thing is he's always got time to chat with people, he's not changed a bit he's still a lovely lad.

ROUND

5

THE FIRST OF THREE CLASSICS!

ON FEBRUARY the 16th 1989 my daughter Carly-Jo was born. Less than a fortnight later I was in the ring with Wally Swift Junior at The York Hall, Bethnal Green over in East London. Wally's record was 15 won, 5 lost and drawn 1. In his corner was his dad and former boxer, Wally Senior, who, if I remember rightly, had held the British Welterweight and Light Middleweight titles in his time. In the crowd that night was Emmanuel Steward from the Kronx gym in New York. He'd trained the likes of Marvellous Marvin Hagler and Thomas "The Hitman" Hearns to name just a couple.

Before the fight Steve Holdsworth, who's now a well known boxing commentator on T V for Eurosport but was then earning a few quid doing his own videos at bouts, would film a show and then sell the tapes for 10 pounds. He was boxing's answer to Richard Branson, a very astute businessman to say the least. Well anyway, he said that Wally Swift Junior wasn't a big puncher and wasn't a banger and that all he had was fast hands. I totally disagreed with that statement and pointed out to him that if any boxer caught you with a good solid shot whoever it was you would feel it. "Never underestimate anyone" I said to him. "If someone catches you on the chin just right you'll go over." And as it happened in the second round of the fight I was put down with a good solid punch. I was moving backwards as he came towards me throwing punches. I was in his corner and slipped on some water which was on the canvas, my right foot went from under me and for a split second it broke my concentration. I looked down and as I've got myself together and gone to throw a jab, then Wally's thrown a right hand over the top and there I am on my arse and that's from someone that's not meant to be much of a puncher. It was a good shot and very accurate. I was back up on me feet in 3 seconds but I don't think my head actually cleared for about 3 hours. I lasted out that round and came on stronger as the fight went on. We were toe to toe most of the fight and head to head banging away at each other, in the 8th Wally stuck the nut on me, but I carried on and didn't complain. Over 8 rounds I think I disheartened him as all of a sudden from being down and nearly out I'd come back and was all over him like a rash but I take nothing away from Wally. I have every respect for him. I was hitting him with shots that should have done him, and would have more then likely finished most other boxers. I was catching him with some unbelievable punches but he kept on coming back. The speed of his recovery was unbelievable. I'd catch him, bang, bang, bang and it would look like I'd had him but he'd come straight back at me and catch me with three or four good shots of his own. He was so durable. In the 8th round as I say he stuck the nut on me and I thought it was deliberate. Anyway, I came out of the clinch with a cut above my eye and a gash underneath it. I think he knew he was behind on points so hence the blatant use of the head, and straight away the ref, Dave Parris, had a good look at it as Harry towelled it down in the corner. "Don't stop the fight Dave, it's the last round" I said to him. He took another look. "He's all right ref," chipped in Harry. "Box on," he said. To tell you the truth the cuts were that bad that if it had of happened earlier on in the fight he would have had no choice but to stop it. I could just about see out of the eye as blood trickled down my face and obscured my vision. My sight was well fucked; I had to keep dabbing at it with my gloves so that I could still see. Afterwards I had eight stitches above the eye and four in the cut below, but all that mattered was that I'd won. It was a hard, tough fight but one that I enjoyed. I loved a battle.

The next morning I was up bright early and out on the milk

round. As I say, a couple of weeks before the fight my daughter was born and I'd be lying if I said it didn't interrupt my preparations. At half past four in the morning, just as I was going out to do my round, Pauline told me that her waters had burst so I got her in the car quickly and sped off down the A40 dual carriageway along the Great Western Avenue heading towards the hospital. She was sitting in the front passenger next to me telling me the baby was on its way, the contractions she was having were getting closer and closer. What I hadn't noticed in the panic was that we'd gone past a police car at about 100mph. I slowed down a bit when I saw their blue, flashing lights come up alongside me. I dropped the window down. "She's having a baby," I shouted, and they could see I wasn't joking by the looks on our faces. They pulled in front of me and escorted me all the way to the hospital with blue lights flashing and sirens wailing. So, I had the new born baby at home keeping me awake, my milk round getting me up at 4.00 a.m. 7 days a week, plus on the side I had a little rubbish clearance business I'd do in an old Ford Transit van I owned. I'd kill two birds with one stone by handing out flyers for my rubbish clearance to all the customers on my milk round. Plus, as soon as I'd finished the milk I'd go out and do some road work, where Id pound the local streets to get my fitness levels higher and build up a bit of strength in my legs. I was a busy little bee who wasn't getting much sleep, not the best way to prepare for a fight. I wasn't back in the ring after the Wally Swift fight for a good 3 months. Harry claimed because of my style he was having problems getting me opponents. I was now getting good reviews in the boxing press, although I was getting called a slugger. But the day after the Swift fight there was an article in the London Evening News about the fight and Emmanuel Stewart who I told you was there, was quoted as saying it was one of the best fights he'd ever seen.

Next up in the June was Tony Britton in a 10 rounder at Battersea Leisure Centre for the vacant Southern Area Light Middleweight Title. He had a bit of an indifferent fight record. He'd won 19, lost 30 and drawn 3. For this fight I upped my road work and would run 8 miles a day in steel toe capped army boots. I thought if it's good enough for the boys in the Paras and the Marines then it was good enough for me. What put that thought in my head I'll never know. I thought if it built my legs up it would build me up. Tony Britton was a black fella that was a bit taller than me and looked a few pounds heavier. He had more experience than me but I was confident of a victory.

In the early rounds he tied me up and frustrated me with his spoiling tactics. He was an awkward customer that would switch from orthodox to southpaw but as I said before, in a fight I get better and stronger as the fight goes on. In the 8th round I caught him and hurt him and the ref jumped in to save him from further punishment. I was now the newly crowned Southern Area champion, and was over the moon. But at the end of the fight I just wanted to put my feet up they were killing me.

Before the fight, I was running in the heavy army hobnailed boots and my feet were killing me. A couple of times I'd got out of bed to go off to do the milk and I'd have to come down the stairs on my bum because my feet were hurting me that much. I was in agony. My feet were throbbing. I just couldn't stand on them. I'd do my milk round in agonizing pain and some days I'd deliver 400 pints of milk. Some of the deliveries were in tower blocks and I was up and down flights of stairs.

After a few weeks I gave up running in the heavy boots and took up cycling. I'd do 25 to 30 mile a night to build my legs and stamina up. I even entered the London to Brighton annual cycle ride along with my wife Pauline who'd also taken up cycling. The fight with Tony Britton had been on the Thursday and the cycle ride was on the Sunday.

On the Monday evening I'd planned a barbeque for family and friends in celebration of winning the title. All was going well on the Sunday bike ride to Brighton when Pauline was knocked off her cycle and broke her kneecap in half. She was taken off to hospital in an ambulance in a right old state. At the hospital the doctors and nurses sorted her out and made her comfortable. I got chatting to the doctor who was attending her and cheekily asked if he could have a look at my feet as they were killing me. I explained that I was a milkman and needed my feet and that also I was a boxer and I'd been doing my road work for a fight in heavy army boots. I told him about not being able to stand up first thing in the morning and that on occasions I'd have to come down the stairs on my bum. "That doesn't sound good," said the doctor, and took me off for some x-rays. Later that day Pauline had her leg in plaster from her ankle to her hip. I came out with her with both me feet in plaster up to my knees. I'd suffered 8 to 10 stress fractures in both feet through running on the roads in them fucking hobnail boots. I'd also been doing my milk round and I'd fought for and won a title, with feet that were fucking killing me and it was no wonder they were. Apparently stress fractures are tiny cracks in the bones but they can cause agony, and didn't I know it.

On the Monday we were both on crutches as 40 odd people turned up at our house for the barbecue. Me and her sat there and watched everyone doing the cooking and getting things organized. I was in plaster for 8 weeks and couldn't work or box. Pauline was in plaster for about 6 weeks. I've been told that stress fractures never fully heal and to this day I still get gyp with them. When Harry and John found out, John came out with some words of wisdom, which he usually did. "You won't do that again will you Andy?" My answer to that was simple and straight to the point. "No John I wont"

For that win I received a belt which is similar in shape and size to a Lonsdale belt but if you are defeated you have to hand it back. I handed it back without defending it. I was out of the ring for 5 months and came back in the November to fight Nigel Fairbairn at Battersea Town Hall. This was his 8th fight and my 12th. He'd won 6, lost 1 and drawn 1 and was a full blown Middleweight. I'd just had 5 months off and to tell the truth was feeling a bit ring rusty even though I'd battled my way back to fitness and sparred countless rounds in the gym. My work in the ring against Fairburn just didn't have snap and sparkle to it but the £800 I was getting for the fight lifted my spirits and it was nice to have a bit of dough in my pocket. I'd been getting a reduced wage on the sick from the dairy and Pauline had only been getting a pittance of sick pay, so money had been tight. We had a mortgage to pay and two kids to feed and clothe.

Two days before that fight I got a really bad head cold and I was bunged up, and couldn't breathe properly, and ached all over. It was the last thing I needed. Anyway, the fight went ahead and it was a real struggle to get going and to get into my rhythm. In the second round I put him on his arse and I should have finished him off in the third. I hurt him and he clung on for dear life. In the 8th round I'd run out of steam and my cold and ring rust were getting the better of me. He was ahead on points so I had to do something drastic. I caught him with a couple of shots and then followed through with my elbow. It was a complete accident but I'd opened up a gaping wound above his eye. The ref took one look and stopped the fight. I never saw Nigel Fairbairn for well over 10 years after our fight but I bumped into him when I was watching boxing ringside one night at the York Hall. He recognized me but to tell you the truth I didn't have a clue who he was. "Do you remember me Andy?" he asked. "We boxed one another." I knew the face but couldn't put a name to it and then it came back to me. "Yeah, I remember I stopped you in the 8th with a cut." "Sorry about the elbow Nigel but you were ahead on points and I couldn't let someone like you beat me." I think he knew where I was coming from and we shook hands and left it at that.

W.O. WILSON
BOXER

I first met Andy Till at the weigh-in for our scheduled fight at Battersea Town Hall on the 29th November 1988. The fight was a complete sell out just two weeks after the tickets went on sale. There was a lot of eyeballing and staring and all that and we were digging each other out with a bit of verbals. I weighed in at 11 stone and Andy at 10st 13lbs and basically we both knew it was going to be a tough fight, no ifs or buts about it. It was going to be that sort of fight.

From the first bell it was just a war. Andy was head butting me quite a bit and the ref was constantly warning him about his head. Andy won the fight on points and when I watched it on tape afterwards the point was made that if the ref had of stopped the fight there would have been a riot. Andy's following seemed to be a mixture of National Front, Chelsea and West Ham football hooligans, even down to members of the riot squad. I'm not taking anything away from Andy but if the fight had of been stopped the gaff would have been smashed up.

I'd heard of Andy before we fought. I was in the Micky Duff, Terry Lawless stable and Andy was with Harry Holland. All the old school, Frank Bruno, Gary Mason, Charlie Magri, Duke Mackenzie were with Micky and Terry when I was there. The Daily Mail described the fight as "a punch up in a telephone box." No one took a step backwards and it was toe to toe. I'd say without doubt Andy was the toughest man I ever met in the ring. I saw Andy a couple of months after the fight and he told me after our fight he stayed in a bath full of water all night because he ached from head to toe. He once lent me his Lonsdale Belt for a photo shoot I was doing and he came along but there was a price to pay. He charged me, the tight git, for the use of it. I think it was 200 pounds he nipped me for. No, I'm just joking. I've the utmost respect for him. We have total respect for one another like a lot of fighters. Things are said before and during fights but afterwards you leave all that behind and become friends.

We still see one another at boxing shows and the odd party and it's always a handshake and a hug. He always pulls my leg about the big female following I had as a boxer.

Later I joined Harry's gym and me and Andy used to have some right tough sparring sessions. I used to catch him with some great body shots and tease him about taking them. I was a bit of a body shot specialist but he still used to come forward pulling that stupid face. No wonder he was nicknamed Stoneface.

Now I work for a company called Gift Point and do gift ideas for feature films. I also have my own fitness company and do fitness classes.

In action as an amateur.

Omma and Oppa, my German grandparents.

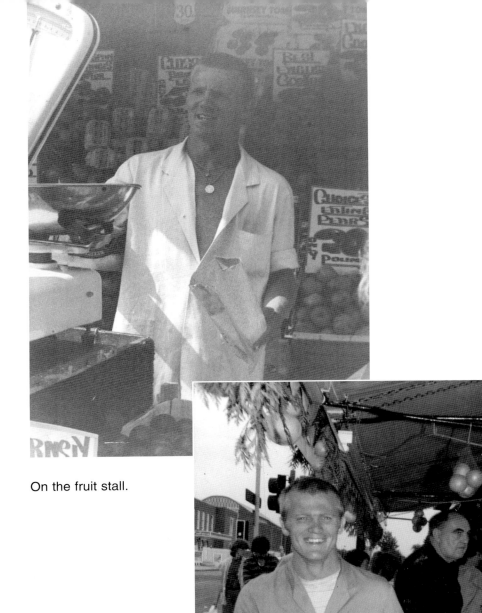

On the fruit stall.

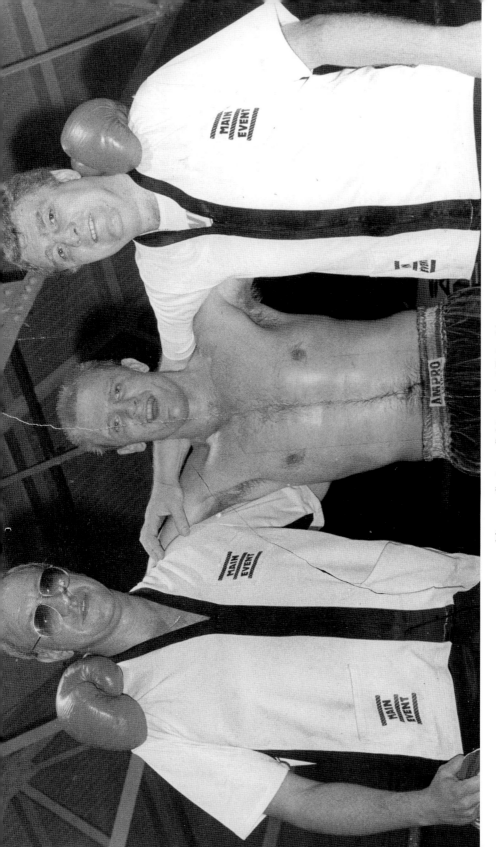

After my first pro fight, against Peter Vance.

Getting a bollocking from Harry.

Seconds out!

Down the gym, posing for the local paper.

Me and W. O. Wilson.
If you can't beat 'em, join
'em.

With Kirkland Lang, who
once beat the great
Roberto Duran.

Southern Area Belt, after beating Tony Brittan.

Sorting out Ensley Bingham before I was disqualified.

Victory over John Davies for the WBC.

Time for a breather, "nice arse".

My youngest son, Jack.

Carly and Jack. don't Jack look like me?

Me and Carly, Daddy's girl.

The look of concentration.

Busy at work.

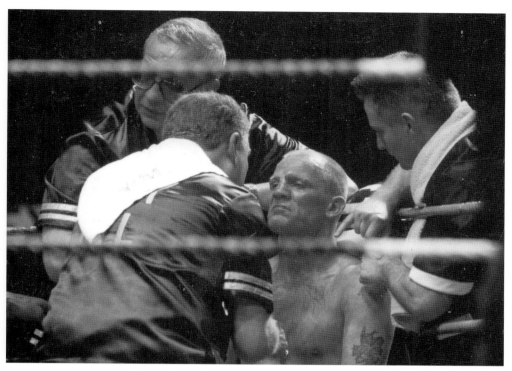

Deep breath and a talking to from Harry.

Some times you have to take one to give one.

Me and the kids.

Jack with my Lonsdale Belt.

ROUND

6

THE SALFORD VIKING

IN MARCH 1990 I was due back at the Battersea Town Hall to take on Winston May, four months after my win over Nigel Fairbairn. But Mr May for one reason or another pulled out of the bout. Steve 'The Viking' Foster, who was on the same bill, also had his opponent pull out so he was going to lose his purse money like me. So I said I'd fight him even though he was a full-blown, middleweight, and I was lighter weight but in the end the match was made. Foster had 19 fights winning 9, losing 9 and one ending in a draw. He was from the highly successful Champs Camp in Manchester's Moss side. My original opponent had pulled out due to medical reasons on the night of the fight. I was more worried about my mortgage getting paid than getting hurt in the ring. The fight was sanctioned by the Boxing Board of Control so I was just glad that I wouldn't be letting my fans down and that I'd be earning a few bob. I weighed in at 11 stone one pound and Foster weighed in at 11 stone 12, but when the weights were announced in the ring I was given as eleven five and Foster as eleven seven, which I'd call cooking the books. You only had to look at him to see he was a lot heavier than me, but the thing was we both wanted the fight.

The first round I got caught by his head and I had my two front teeth knocked out. Well they never actually came out; they got loosened and stuck in the roof of my mouth. I just wanted the first round to end so that John, in my corner could take a look at the damage. It was bothering me and was uncomfortable to say the least. John took out my gum shield and pulled out the two loose teeth. In the second round I go to throw a jab and he counters with a big right hand over the top and I'm laying flat on my back. It was a good shot that caught me flush on the chin. I'm back on my feet on the count of four and the ref lets us box on. He catches me again and I take it and we move around the ring. He moves in again, throws another big shot and over I go again. I get back to my feet and he moves in to finish me off. The ref has allowed us to box on and Foster comes towards me with the most stupid swagger I've ever seen. He was so cocky, like he'd done the job already. He had his arms down by his side and his shoulders were rolling from side to side and he bounced towards me full of attitude. My head cleared and I hung on for dear life until the ref told me to let go. He'd break us and order us to box on. "I'll give you swagger towards me you flush cunt," I'm thinking.

In the third and fourth rounds I fucking mullered him. I battered him and some of my body shots were breaking him in half. As I was catching him up the ribs I could hear him groaning. "Aaaahhhh," I heard him murmur as my gloves sunk deep into his body. I knew I had him. He wasn't so flash now. He did catch me again in the 4th and I held onto him again until my head cleared and I got back to work knocking the granny out of him. I thought the ref would stop the fight in this round because I was all over him like a rash. The ref was Ritchie Davies, a good and very fair ref. Some refs would have called a halt to the fight with my second knock down, but the ref knew I came on stronger as the fight went on and he knew Foster was a strong lad that could take a punch and come back from it. He knew each of our strengths.

At the end of the 5th round the ref was called over to Foster's corner and told that their fighter wasn't coming out for the 6th due to a damaged hand which to me was a load of bollocks. I'd broken his heart not his hand. After the fight there was talk between Fosters manager Phil Martin and Harry of a re-match at the G-Mex Centre in Manchester for a title fight, but nothing ever come of it. In his corner at Battersea that night doing the water bucket and sponge was Ensley Bingham who was to be my next opponent.

I was due to meet Bingham back at Battersea Town Hall 3 months after the Foster fight and the bout was to be the final eliminator for the British title. Bingham had watched me batter his mate from Manchester all around the ring at close quarters, and he knew he was going to have his work cut out. Bingham was a good solid fighter who could bang a bit. He'd had 9 fights winning 5 and losing 4. The ref was John Coyle who was from Bingham's neck of the woods. In the first round Bingham cut me above the left eye with a deliberate butt. In the second round he catches me above the right eye and cuts me again. I'm now cut over both eyes and the ref hasn't said a word to him about the use of his head. I take all this in my stride and start getting to work behind some good solid jabs and hooks. I catch him with a good body shot and he doubles up. He then springs up and catches me well below the belt with a left and right hook to my bollocks. I did no more than elbow him straight in the back of the head. I smashed him so hard in the back of the neck I swear I was trying to break it. Three times he'd got away with deliberate fouls and had not been warned. My blood was boiling. We were told to both cut it out and to box on, and with that he comes in close and nuts me on the cheek and then on the chin. I was fucking fuming. I pushed him down and he was bent over double and as he's leaning over I try to bring my elbow with real force down onto the back of his neck. I wanted to hurt him badly but I missed him but the ref instantly disqualified me. He shouldn't have done really because technically I hadn't touched him. I got back to my corner and got an almighty bollocking from Harry and John about my behaviour. I was going fucking mad. I'm no angel and I know I've taken a few liberties in the ring in my time, but he was taking the piss. I was that incensed I didn't go over to his corner at the end of the fight. Traditionally you're, supposed to go to your opponent's corner and shake hands with their corner men. The crowd, were going mental and it looked like it was going to kick off outside the ring. I even had to get on the M.C.'s mike and appeal for a bit of calm. Things were getting heavy and you could cut the atmosphere with a flick knife.

Foster went on to fight Ronald Winky Wright and so did Bingham, and if I remember rightly he battered the pair of them. Bingham later fought Wally Swift for the British Title and got knocked out in the 4th round.

A few days later I received a letter from the Boxing Board of Control about my behaviour in the ring against Bingham. Me and Harry had to attend a meeting in front of the Board. I was found guilty of misbehaving and half of my £1,500 purse was withheld. I pleaded my innocence but I was still found guilty. There were pictures of me doing my wrestling moves on him in a couple of the daily tabloids, which did nothing to help my cause. I said at first that the bloke pictured in the papers was my brother and I kept a right straight face as I pleaded my innocence. The members of the boxing board present stayed unmoved and their expressions never changed at my attempt to bring some humour to the proceedings. The panel was not impressed with my exploits and let it be known, so I explained that I'd been head butted and punched below the belt, but my words fell on deaf ears, not so much cauliflower ears, because how many of these people who were deciding my future had ever pulled on a pair of boxing gloves? Along with the fine I was put back 12 months in my quest for a title. In fact it put me back nearly two years before I got a shot at it, but in less than 3 months after the Bingham fight I was back at Battersea Town Hall to face Alan Richards. He'd fought as a Welterweight against my stable mate, Trevor Smith, who'd knocked him out in 6 rounds, so he was now getting in with me and trying his luck as a Light Middleweight. I was all over him but somehow he managed to weather the storm and stay on his feet. I had him down in the first round but give him his due, he held on and was very brave. It turned out to be just another day at the office and I ended up winning an 8 round points decision.

Five months later we met again at surprise, surprise, Battersea Town Hall. That was the 5th time on the trot I'd fought there. Since we last met Richards had fought another 4 times and now boasted a pro record of 8 wins, 7 losses and one draw. I'd had quite a long lay off out of the ring and he'd been busy keeping himself fit and taking a few fights. I was really back in the ring again with Richards because it was simple. No one else would fight me. Harry was having problems getting me opponents, not because I was some superman fighter or that I was some tremendous boxer, it was because win or lose, my opponents knew they'd be in for a tough fight. Back in the ring with Richards, I battered him, for 8 rounds but credit where credits due he took everything I threw at him and stayed on his feet for the 8 rounds. But it was an easy points win.

After about four months out of the ring I was matched with Irish Champion Terry Magee. Magee had done an article in The Boxing News stating that I shouldn't be the number 1 contender for the British Light Middleweight Title and that he should be. Well, like a little school kid I got the hump with him saying that and a few weeks later I replied in print saying that if he thought that then let's get the fight on. So that was it. The match was made and the fight went ahead at London's York Hall, Bethnal Green. Magee had plenty of experience and had a record of 20 wins, 5 losses and 1 draw. This was to be my 17th pro fight and it was up to me to prove that I was the real worthy number 1 challenger.

I'd kept myself reasonably fit during my lay off but 6 weeks before the fight I really got back into my training and never felt better. My sparring had gone well, my road work all done, and I felt sharp and confident. Leading up to the fight me and Pauline and the two kids had moved from our small but cozy Bovis home to a smart larger three bedroom semi over in Hayes. I really thought I'd made it. The place, or my palace, even had a downstairs extension. Not bad for a snotty nosed kid from a council estate?

On the night the York Hall was packed to the rafters and the place was rocking. To add spice to the insults traded between us before the fight we were then told that this was to be a final elimination for the right to fight the then champion, Wally Swift Junior, for his title, but due to some controversy or other and a bit of boxing politics it turned out that the bout was just a straight contest with nothing but pride at stake. I just wanted to get out there and bash him for what he'd said about me. From the first bell I got out there and took charge. The BBC was recording the fight for Grandstand, which would be shown on a Saturday afternoon before the football results. I caught him with a good solid shot and opened up bad cut above his eye. I done everything to make it worse. I rubbed my head it it, elbowed him, I done everything to make him feel uncomfortable. I would have kneed him in the eye if I could have got away with it.

In the 3rd round he had a lump come up on his other eye the size of a tennis ball. I used him as a punch bag and battered the fuck out of him. How this bloke had beaten Wally Swift Junior I'll never know. The ref stepped in and stopped him from further punishment in the 4th and if he hadn't I would have ended up knocking him out and hurting him. I went over to him in his corner as he sat on his stool looking glum and battered. He looked up at me and half smiled. "Who should be number 1 now then?" I asked. There was no reply. I gave him a little tap on the head and walked back to my corner. Afterwards I sat at home and watched one of Steve Holdsworth's home videos of the fight and I don't know what fight he was watching but it certainly wasn't the fight with Magee. "Magee has Till in trouble here," you can hear him screaming excitedly on the tape. "A good left and right from Magee as Till is under pressure." I'd heard enough I stopped the video and phoned him. "Oi Steve, what the fuck are you on about, you must have been watching a different fight to the one I've just been in," I said. He tried to laugh it off and make light of it and tried to joke about it. "I'll tell you something Steve," I said. "If you ever commentate on another fight of mine like that again you will find out just how good a boxer I really am." To this day we're still friends and as I say, Steve now has a plum job commentating on the boxing for Eurosport.

JOHN HOLLAND
BOXING TRAINER

I was about 11 when I first met Andy. I was fighting his Northolt club mate, Brian Nichols, and Andy was fighting my club mate, Rocky Kelly. Me and Brian had three fights between us and they were pretty competitive and Andy and Rocky had 4 fights which were proper wars. There's a bit of debate as to how many fights Andy and Rocky had with each other. Andy and my dad say they had three but I remember them having 4 with them each winning two apiece. My first impression of Andy was just how tough he was. I'd nowadays put him up there with the Lenny McLean and Roy Shaws of this world.

Andy as a youngster was the toughest kid on the block, no doubt about it. When he turned pro I followed his career and I knew he was going to be a better pro than he was an amateur. He just had that style that suited the pro game. My Dad, Harry, encouraged Andy to fight that way. Out of the ring he's a good mate of mine but he's the most genuine geezer you could ever meet. He looks menacing and looks the part and he is the part, only a fool would want to cross swords with him. He's put on weight since he stopped boxing and his shoulders are massive, but he still carries himself well and he's a big intimidating man. He's never been a bully but has had a few scrapes in the past. I never did turn pro but I know a great fighter when I see one and one of the greats was definitely Andy. I now run my own boxing gym in Hounslow, West London. It's called The Westside Gym and I've got pro and amateur fighters there.

ROUND

7

AN INTERNATIONAL BELT
UNDER MY BELT

IN OCTOBER 1991 I fought John Davies at the Town Hall in Dudley, which is in the West Midlands, for the WBC International Belt. This belt and title is for fighters outside of the worlds top ten in their weight division, but inside the top thirty list of fighters. The holder of this belt then gets the automatic chance of a shot at the WBC World Champion. John Davies was a good, strong boxer who had moved up from Welterweight. The fight was over 12 rounds which is a fucking long time. That's 36 minutes of boxing.

I was still doing my milk round and doing my rubbish clearance, but things had gone a bit quiet on that front. That was until I get a call from a little Indian fella over in Southall. It was one of them houses where you come straight out the front door and onto the pavement. There was no front garden. He'd knocked all the walls down inside and made it all open plan, but all the rubble and bricks and bits of wood and shit he'd stored in a pile outside in the back garden. It was a terraced house, the sort you'd see on Coronation Street. I told him there was probably three full van loads and that once I'd loaded the truck up he was to pay me then to take it away. We agreed a price and I got to work wheeling barrow loads of the builders' rubbish out and tipping it onto the truck. I had sheets of ply up the side so that I could get more on board. I loved the hard work and it helped with my training. It took me a couple of hours to load up the first lot and before I left to take it to Greenford dump, the man paid me. It was fucking hard graft. Greenford was a council run tip but I knew a couple of fellas that worked there that would let me dump my rubbish for a tenner a load. They made it easier for me by bulldozing the rubbish off the back of the truck with the big shovel. All was going well. I went back to the house and done the second load, and got paid and done the same down the dump, bunged the boys their drink and went back for the third load. I loaded that up and asked the bloke for the final bit of money.

"Me have no more money," said the man.

"Don't tell me that, I've told you it's 100 pounds a load and you've only paid for two," I said.

"No more money mate," he said, shaking his head.

"I'm going to give you the chance to get your money or something drastic is going to happen," I told him, with steam now coming out of my ears.

"I have no more money," he said, so I picked up half a paving slab and threw it straight through the glass on his brand new double glazed front door.

"That's just for starters," I growled. "Don't take the piss out of me."

I then told him that I was going to reverse the fully laden truck through the front wall and into his lounge. I jumped into the motor, turned the engine on and slammed the gears into reverse.

"Wait, wait," he shouted, as I got to within 6 inches of the house. I put the brakes on but left the engine revving.

"I've got the money, I've got the money," he shouted.

"I thought you might have," I said, as I switched off the engine.

I'm not racist but I won't let anyone take the piss out of me no matter what colour their skin is.

It was the same on my milk round. Some people would not pay their milk bill for weeks, sometimes even months, but I gave them the benefit of the doubt and still left them their daily pinta even though they was avoiding opening their front doors to settle their bills. I knew they were inside as sometimes I could see them sitting in their kitchens or sitting on their settees watching the telly, totally ignoring me ringing their front door bell or rattling their letter boxes. Some people have no shame and would think nothing of mugging me off. I delivered 2 pints of milk for over two months to these four Paddy fellas that were renting a house on an estate I delivered on. The bill was going up and up and they would totally ignore me. I could see them walking about inside through their glass front door but do you think they'd open up and settle their bill? One morning I'd had enough and banged the letter box about 100 times and kicked the glass at the bottom of the door. I could see someone inside rushing along the hallway towards me and the front door flew open.

"What the fuck are you doing knocking my front door like that for?' said a huge Irishman, his face red with rage.

"I've been knocking on this door for the last 5 weeks and you've ignored me," I told him.

"There's no need to be knocking on me door like that because you're going the right way to be getting a slap," he says.

"Is that right?" I said, and with that I've done him with a right hander. He's fell forward onto the path and I've grabbed him and rubbed his face up and down the pebble dashing on the front wall. A second one's come out and I've gone bang, bang, and done him. The first one I hit then started to come round, so I've started back with him, the second one gets back up and now we're all fighting in the front garden where the grass must be 3 ft long and all me pound coins and loose change is coming out of me leather money bag and going everywhere. A third one appears and then a fourth.

"Leave it, leave it," one of them shouts, and he calms it all down.

"I didn't want no grief, I just want paying," I said. "I was good enough to leave you milk so now be good enough to pay me," and with that one of them did.

I got back to the yard after my round and the Old Bill were there waiting for me. I was questioned about the incident and they wanted to know what had gone on. I asked them if they thought I was stupid enough to start trouble with four huge Paddies who had threatened to smash my face in. They'd taken liberties with me, they told me not to knock again because if I did they would smash my face in, one of them 'as lost his temper and taken a swing at me and the others have joined in. I was only defending myself. Also I've lost over £130 worth of change when they all piled out of the house and man handled me into the grass in the front garden. I'm the one that's lost out here I told the Old Bill. They weren't too happy though because a couple of the Paddies were badly injured and I didn't have a mark on me but in anyone's book surely four onto one ain't fair. I never heard any more but the dairy covered my losses and I never delivered to the house again. One house I went to nearly every morning was Wiggy and Joan Puddles, who were, me mate Tony Puddles Mum and Dad. I'd get around there about 5-30 in the morning and the front door would be unlocked and ajar for me and I'd go in and Wiggy would be up and would do me a cup of milky tea and a couple of rounds of hot buttered toast. He worked on a fruit and veg stall and was always up early so we'd always sit in the kitchen and have a tea and a bit of a natter, he was a right nice geezer. One morning I turned up and pushed the door and it was locked I banged on the door and Joanie came down " Where's Wiggy the lazy bastard" I joked.

"I think he's having a layin " she said " I think he's tired"

"Well fucking get him up because he'll be late for work" She's gone up stairs and she starts shouting and screaming " Wiggy, Wiggy wake up I can't go on without my Wiggy, I can't live without my Wiggy." She's come running past me on the stairs as I was on my way up and ran into the kitchen and slammed the door shut. Behind their kitchen door was a magnetic knife holder, which was full of sharp knives of all description. "I can't live without my Wiggy" she's screaming so I had visions of her behind the kitchen door holding one of these knives and about to harm herself, so booted the door in and ran in and picked her up in a fireman's carry and carried her to her sisters house next door. I phoned Tony and told him there was a problem at his Mum and Dads place, he came straight over and when he turned up I told him straight that his Dad was dead, there was no easy way to tell him.

On the day of the fight with Davies, me Harry and John traveled up there by car. We got to the venue and I sorted out all my boxing gear. Once that was done I found a quiet corner and had a kip as usual. I was never one for looking around the empty venue or bouncing or skipping about in the ring. While everyone was rushing around John would bandage my hands up and Id be off in the land of nod. I had 3 coach loads of supporters coming up from London for this fight. Davies was a pumped up Welterweight that had knocked over nearly all his opponents. He'd had 15 fights with just one loss so he had a fair old record and by all accounts he could box and bang a bit.

The fight was about evens for the first 4 rounds and he was one strong fucker. In the 5th he nutted me with his head and cut me, which later required 8 stitches. He was an awkward fighter but in the end my strength took over and I won fair and square and Davies knew that. I beat him on points over 12 rounds but it was a hard fought battle. I received my W.B.C. belt in the ring and held it aloft to show it off to my fans and the T.V. cameras that were there.

The next day I watched a tape of the fight at home and ex-world champion, Jim Watt, was the commentator. Fuck knows what fight he was watching. I sat there listening to his comments on how the fight was panning out. You must have left your glasses at home that night Jim. But he did comment at the end that I was just that bit too strong for Davies so you wasn't entirely wrong Jimbo.

The next day I was up the gym to collect my purse money from Harry. I think I got about three grand for that fight but out of that I had to pay him 25% of my earnings. I knew it was a business to him and he was in it for one thing and that was to make money. He certainly wasn't in it for his health or fitness but saying that, he always had my best interests at heart and he's a great fella and to this day still a good friend. If I needed him he'd be straight round and likewise vice-versa.

TONY PUDDLE
GREENGROCER

I've known Andy about 30 years and we grew up as kids together and hung around Northolt as young chaps. He was working on the greengrocers, stall for Chick and I was doing the same but for someone else. I used to go and watch all of Andy's amateur fights and as he got older and turned pro I followed him then.

As a person he's a nice guy and a very close friend to all my family. When he used to do his milk round he used to pop into my mum and dad's and have a cup of tea with them. They'd treat him like a son. One day he turned up at their home and mum told Andy she was having trouble waking the old man up. Andy went upstairs to get him out of bed and it turns out me Dad had died in his sleep. He stayed with my mum and comforted her until help arrived and it was sorted out and he showed at times like that what a good heart he's got.

Another time my younger brother was getting something out of our garage and as he lifted the up and over door open it came down on his head and nearly split him in half. There was blood everywhere but Andy was indoors at the time and by chance he found him and took him up the hospital to get it sorted out and stitched. Andy even told the nurse stitching him up how to do it. He told her to keep the stitches small and close together so when it healed he wouldn't have much of a scar. Good old Doctor Till! He always seemed to be there, it was uncanny. I don't now if it was luck or what. I don't know what it is but he was always there at the right time.

Even today he treats my kids as his own and over the years he's been a really good friend. As a kid he had a hard life at home and I don't remember many kids wanting to start trouble with him. You wouldn't would

Getting to work with the heavy bag, down the gym.

Three Southern Area champions from the same stable.
Me, light middleweight; Trevor Smith, welterweight; Serge Fame, light heavyweight.

British Boxing Board of Control Ltd

I confirm that I have today carried out the following medical examination test

on .... Andrew Till ....

DR. C. N. SAWYER
48 WIMPOLE STREET
LONDON W1M 7DG
071-935 4357

Delete as applicable :-

1. Medical examination
2. Ophthalmic examination
3. Skull x-ray
4. CT Scan
5. Other (please state) ....

THE HARLEY STREET SCANNING CENTRE
42 HARLEY STREET, LONDON W1N 1AB
Dr. BRIAN KENDALL   Dr. IVAN MOSELEY
Dr. RICHARD MASON Dr. ALAN VALENTINE
TEL: 580 3213

I confirm the applicant/boxer has produced passport sized photographs which
I have countersigned, or his boxing licence as proof of identity.

Signed ....   11.02.94.

Stamp

DR. C. N. SAWYER
48 WIMPOLE STREET
LONDON W1M 7DG
...757

THE HARLEY STREET SCANNING CENTRE
42 HARLEY STREET, LONDON W1...
Dr. BRIAN KENDALL   Dr. IVAN MOSELEY
Dr. RICHARD MASON Dr. ALAN VA...
TEL: 580 3213

British Boxing
Board of Control
Ltd. Medical
examination test
certificate, 1994.

Me and Johnny Bloomfield.

After this photo Harry coined the name 'Stone Face'.

I trained for the Bingham fight out in Marbella. Here I'm taking a break with my daughter Carly.

Me as Hanibal Lector.

'Gather round boys, let me tell you just how good I am.'
This picture was taken at my brother's scout camp for the local paper.

Me, cashing in after winning the British title
Next 2 pages: The Tony Collins fight. He had no answer, I mullered him.

(*above*) Me and Wally Swift get to it. We had three great fights.

(*right*) Me and Wally Swift Jnr. after a bruising battle.

(*facing page*) Lonsdale Belt and my WBC International belt.

Me and Butterscotch
doing a Clint Eastwood.

Pauline and me. 'Mind
you don't fall, love.

Me and Pauline after a fight, before we started fighting.

Me and Wally in action, he was as game as fuck.

ya? The man's a freak of nature. I've seen him get hit in the ring with shots that would put a horse down but Andy still keeps coming. It must be like hitting a brick wall. You just can't hurt him. Nothing matters to him in the ring.

I still work on the fruit stalls over at Ealing in West London and I speak to Andy at least once a week on the phone. He's a top fella.

ROUND

SECOND HELPINGS OF WALLY

AFTER the John Davies bout I was out of the ring for nearly a whole year before I met my old adversary Wally Swift Jr. again for the British Light Middleweight Title. The fight was held at Watford just north of London.

I also had another addition to the Till family, my son Jack, who was born on the 16th February and shares a birthday with my daughter Carly-Jo.

Wally had won the title from Ensley Bingham who he knocked out in 8 rounds. I'd been disqualified against Bingham for elbowing him in the back of the head. This fight with Wally was my 19th pro fight and Swift's 34th pro fight. Wally had just suffered a defeat at the hands of Jean Claude Fontana for the European crown and had undergone surgery on his troublesome eye tissue. Through out his career Wally had been prone to cuts around his eyes. In the run up to the fight I'm doing all my usual training and I'm still on the milk and flying around my round like a nutter keeping fit. Don't worry about Benny Hill and Ernie. I was the fastest milkman in the west!

One night I was sparring with Barry Ellis, a big black heavy-weight. He threw a right hand and I blocked it with my elbow but I felt like an electric shock shoot up my arm. I've never felt pain like it. I was in fucking agony. I pulled up straight away and went back to the corner where Harry took a look at it. "That's all right," he said and we carried on sparring. At the end of the session there was a lump the size of an orange on my elbow and it hurt like fuck. I ignored it for a few weeks thinking it was just badly bruised. Me and Barry had some tough, rough rounds of sparring over the weeks leading up to the fight. He was a big bruiser of a heavyweight and when he caught you with a shot it hurt, but there were times when I wobbled him with some good shots. He was about 4 stone heavier than me and had lost as many as he'd won in the pro game. He could have been an extremely good fighter but he was just a little lazy and at times he'd just go through the motions and was ponderous, but he packed a powerful punch and knew the fight game well so we had some good battles in the ring. I also sparred with Serge Fame who was a light heavyweight who'd fought for the British Title and he again was also a very good and clever boxer and a lovely fella. One night when we were in the ring he hit me with an upper cut which caught me right on the tip of my nose and nearly took my nose off my face. I ended up going to hospital and having 12 stitches put in and they sewed back the piece of flesh and bone that separates the nostrils. It was the part of the nose that the Eastenders actress, Danielle Westbrooke, had missing, but hers was from chang abuse and mine was from pleasure. I think pop star David Bowie had a similar problem to Danielle's in the 70s but I think his was from his life on Mars or some planet he was on at the time.

This all happened just three weeks before the fight with Swift and I was in agony. At the hospital they tried to give me an anaesthetic near to the injury but the needle just came straight through my nostrils and out the other side. My septum, the dividing partition inside my nostrils, had been ripped to pieces. I ended up having 12 stitches, 8 inside the nose and 4 underneath. I didn't really feel a thing as they patched me up as my adrenaline was pumping.

The next day I was back in the gym skipping and doing a light work out and within two days I was back sparring. Johnny B found this huge Hannibal Lector type headwear from somewhere and strapped it on my head. I wore this massive head guard that weighed about 10lb in old money. I looked like Frankenstein or John 'the elephant man 'Merrick, as I dragged myself around the ring with this huge contraption balanced on my nut this thing was like a jousting mask. It was so heavy. Leading up to the fight it seemed nothing was going my way. It seemed to be one thing after another. I'd had all the trouble with my elbow, which was still swollen, but with still no idea what was causing the pain. I'd been up what seemed every night with the new baby teething and having to be changed, fed and watered and now what with losing half me hooter, I didn't feel a million dollars. I thought Harry was maybe thinking about pulling me out of the fight. I told him I was carrying on regardless as there was no way he was going to pull me out and there was no way I'd throw the towel in. The fight was to be shown on Sky T.V. and I was earning 36 grand, the highest purse I'd received for a fight. I was no quitter and the dough was just too good to turn down. I'd be there even if I had to crawl into the ring. I'd gone from £1500 for my last fight with John Davis to 36 grand for this bout. I was rubbing my hands together. In my eyes I was a very rich man. I think Wally was getting 36 grand for the fight as well and he was the champion.

On the day of the fight I was buzzing. We had the weigh in about 2.30 p.m. at the Town Hall and then we went to a hotel around the corner and chilled out. We all knew it was going to be a hard fight. The last fight had been a lot harder than any of us had thought and this time the fight was scheduled for 12 rounds. I was confident I could go the distance and do 12 rounds if need be. The ref came in and gave his instructions and told me what he expected of me but to tell you the truth I wasn't really taking a lot of notice. I'd not long woke up after me pre fight nap and I'm a bit of a miserable bastard when I first wake up, plus I just wanted to get in the ring, hear that first bell and get to it. When it was time to leave the dressing room I followed Johnny Bloomfield out with my gloved hands on his shoulders. Harry followed behind rubbing my neck muscles. I could hear the crowd roaring and shouting but I wasn't paying much attention. It was like a rumble, a wall of noise. I got into the ring with a good sweat on and with the raving hump. After I lost my front teeth against Steve Foster I had a special gum shield made which fitted the gaps in my teeth. Also the towel I had around my neck when I got into the ring would be the one I'd used to dry my kids with after I'd bathed them before I set off for the fight. So when I walked into the ring I could smell and feel my children with me on the towel. It was something I'd done for a while but on the day of the fight some low life cunt had nicked my gum shield and my special towel out of my bag. I was fucking livid. I was spitting feathers. The two things meant a hell of a lot to me for obvious reasons. I found out about 3 hours before the fight that the things were missing. The gum shield had been especially made by a dentist and had cost me £100 and the towel was priceless. I ended up borrowing a gum shield off of someone else and packed a load of bubblegum around it and shaped it around my mouth so the gum filled in where my missing teeth should be. I then stuck in in the freezer and let it get semi hard. I had, and still have, my suspicions on who took my gear and the slimey no good cunt half thinks I know it was him and one day it will be pay back time you fucking rat faced cunt. I have a name and a face in my mind of who done it and I'm just biding my time. What goes around comes around. I'd even phoned home just to check to see if I'd left them behind by mistake but they weren't there it was obvious the things had been nicked out of my bag. Normally before I got into the ring I'd limber up a bit and stretch my muscles and limbs and get warmed up on the pads with Johnny, but this was so different. I knew I couldn't afford a slow start so by the time I climbed through them ropes I was ready to explode. I noticed my wife Pauline and my brothers Peter, Raymond and John and sister Anna sitting in the crowd. They came to most of my fights and there was no way I was going to let them down.

The bell sounded for the first round and we carried on how we finished our last fight, with both of us steaming into one another and exchanging some good solid shots. There was no real bad blood between me and Wally although I got the impression his old man didn't like me much but that didn't stop us knocking the shit out of each other. We went toe to toe for the first few rounds and I'd say I won them all and don't forget I was carrying that injury to my elbow but only my training camp knew that as it wasn't common knowledge. In the 5th round Wally caught me with a hard shot which bounced off the side of my head. Almost immediately he dropped his hand down by his side. I knew straight away he'd hurt himself as he winced in pain and let out a puff of air from his open mouth. From then on for some reason I didn't use my right hand on him. I started boxing one handed subconsciously. I must have thought it unfair that Wally was at a disadvantage with only one hand. In the corner at the end of the 8th Harry told me a few home truths and told me to get my act together because I was in danger of throwing this fight away because I was being stupid by boxing with one hand. That talking to kick started me back into fighting again and I took charge of the fight as I swarmed all over Wally and won the fight on points. But it was close. It turns out that Wally had broken his hand in the 3rd round but battled on bravely to the end Imagine what the fight would have been like if both of us had been a 100% fit? Now I was British Light Middleweight Champion, I was on course to fulfill my dream of winning a Lonsdale belt outright.

A few weeks later I was told that both Wally and me had won an award for that fight and we were to receive a trophy for the Fight of the Year. It was a great honour because there had been some great British fights that year and we'd beaten the likes of Lennox Lewis and Frank Bruno and Michael Watson, Nigel Benn, Chris Eubank in winning this award. I sat next to Lennox that night and he was a ;proper gent. A few years later I met Frank Bruno at one of Audley Harrison's fights and he came over to me and said "Andy, did I box you once?" I laughed. "Leave it out Frank, you were about 5 weights heavier than me." He looked at me blankly and that was the end of that.

Almost immediately after the Swift fight Harry had agreed with Frank Warren for me to meet Tony Collins for the British Title I'd just won from Wally Swift. Collins was a travelling boy who I believed had had a manufactured career in as much that his opponents were selected very carefully for him. Facing me in the ring was a huge step up in class for him. He'd had 26 wins, 3 losses and 1 draw but he'd never ever come up against anyone like me. His brother George had had a fantastic amateur career but never really made it as a pro. The fight was made for the 12 of December 1992 at The York Hall, Bethnal Green and it promised to be a classic.

About 6 weeks before the fight Collins was in The Boulevard Nightclub in Ealing, West London. Quite a few of my mates drunk in there and one of them got talking to Collins about the fight. Collins told my mate, Mick Campion, to get me down to the club and that me and him could have it bare knuckle on the cobbles outside the club. Mick phoned me at 1.30 a.m. at home and told me Collins was at the club and was bad mouthing me. I was in bed with the wife sound asleep when he phoned and had to be up at 4.00 a.m. for me milk round. Collins came on the phone and told me I was a coward and that I should get my arse down to the club and have it with him on the cobbles. "Do fucking what?" I shouted down the phone to him, and jumped out of bed and started to get dressed. He had got my goat up and I was fuming. They've got some fucking front them gypsy boys. I knew I'd knock him all around Ealing when I got hold of him, the saucy cunt. As I pulled my trousers on Pauline woke up and asked me what I was doing and what all the shouting was about. "That was Tony Collins and he's up at the nightclub in Ealing and he wants to fight me now," I told her. She turned over. "Get back to bed Andy, you're fighting him in a few weeks, don't be so silly." I stopped and thought for a few seconds and took my strides off and slipped back into the warm sheets. An hour later the phone went again and it was Collins. I listened to what he had to say and then told him "let's get the fight in the ring out of the way and then we'll fight on the cobbles for the whole purse of the fight with the winner taking all." He agreed and I thought "that's fucking lovely, I'll have some of that." I'd be only too willing to put my share of the purse up.

As I was preparing for the fight with Collins I noticed a few gypsy fellas coming down the gym to watch me train. I half knew Joe Smith one of the blokes through Johnny B, but weren't too sure whether they'd come down to spy on me. Anyway, one night I pulled them up and asked them what was going on. It turns out they weren't too keen on the Collins clan and Joe offered his services as my sparring partner. Joe was around fifteen stone and he was a hard man, anyway we ended up sparing many rounds and he had strength and power and technically was very good. He took a lot of good shots off me and I had the utmost respect for him. His cousin, Jimmy Stockin, is the legendary bare knuckle fighter and Jimmy's younger brother, Wally, was also a handy fighter inside and outside the ring. So, I had some good boys on my side and I have total respect for them. Years later me and Joe fell out over a debt collecting job where when he paid me out my share I was 20 quid light. I take earning money very serious and I don't like being ripped off or short changed. He claimed he was only messing around but I know them traveling boys like to try it on and take a few liberties if you let them. But since then I'm pleased to say we've made it up and are now the best of friends again. I like Joe and his family so it wasn't nice falling out with him.

During the build up to the Collins fight I still had that badly swollen elbow and at times I was in agony with it and still hadn't been to the doctors to have it checked out. The fight was on Sky T.V. and the place was packed for the first defense of my title. The atmosphere was electric and if anything my supporters were that bit louder than the braces and dealer boot brigade, many of them with the Bryl-creamed Elvis look hair. It was more Graceland than Eastend. The Collins family came from Yateley in Surrey and some of the things they got up to were legendary. The tales of what they'd done and hadn't done certainly made me laugh although most of it was probably a load of bollocks. You know what travelers are like when it comes to telling a story. The same as when you hear how long some of these bare knuckle fights have gone on for. 2 hours? 3 hours? 4 hours? Who times these fights? I don't think I've ever seen a gypsy with a watch on and most of them have no perception of time.

The fight was scheduled for 12 x 3 minute rounds. The first round I just walked straight through all his shots and refused to be hurt by him. I fucking hammered him. I wasn't pussy-footing around. The second round I carried on the same way, just coming forward and taking the fight to him. I took the middle of the ring while all he was doing was moving off or holding. "Keep still ya cunt so that I can hit you," I said as I got into a clinch with him. I then caught him with a good right hand and his legs buckled, his head flopped forward and the pony tail his hair was tied up in hit me in the face. I blinked as his hair went in my eyes. I grabbed hold of him and physically threw him across the ring and he landed on the floor. "Get off me ya fucking mug," I shouted at him as he looked up at me from the canvas. I got a right telling off of the ref who was none too pleased with my antics. "Sorry ref," I said, and the bell sounded for the end of the second. He looked a bit shook up and a bit jittery as he made his way back to his corner.

He now knew just how determined and strong I actually was. We came out for the third and I had no respect for him. I wanted to hurt and humiliate him, after he'd tried to show me up in front of my pals in the nightclub. Before the fight I'd done an interview with the Boxing News and told them it would be "a man against a boy" and I was so right. Early in the round we went toe to toe and he caught me with what he must have thought were decent body shots. I held my gloves up to the side of my head, lifted my elbows out to my sides and said "have another go you mug, they're no good." I then laughed at him. "Is that all you've got you mug," I added, and by the look on his face I knew he was disheartened. He'd had enough. I then opened up on him, bang, bang, bang. My shots bounced off his face and as his head jerked back, beads of sweat sprayed off his contorted features. I had him. He tried to cover up but a strong right hand blasted through on to the top of his nut and down he went. He had the count but got back up and I tore straight back into him. I steamed in with lefts and rights and it was only the ropes holding him up. He then sat on the middle rope with me all over him like a rash. I was knocking the granny out of him. He was crumbling under the pressure. The ref let him get upright without giving him another count and we boxed on. He danced around the ring with me chasing him. I caught up with him and hit him with half a dozen shots. He was well and truly fucked as the ref stepped in and stopped the fight. As he was lead back to his corner he looked over his shoulder at me. I gave him the wankers sign. "Andy, Andy, what you doing that for?" asked Johnny Bloomfield, a bit concerned at my behaviour, but I hadn't told them about the nightclub fiasco with Collins. I'd kept it all to myself. I walked over to his corner. He was a broken, defeated boy as he lay half slumped over the top rope. The taste of defeat stuck in his big mouth.

"Still fancy it outside on the cobbles?" I asked.

"Nah" he replied.

"You mug" I said as I tapped him on the back of the head with my glove.

"I didn't think you would, you cunt" I added, and I strolled back to my corner delighted at my nights work. It was a stroll in the park as I'd predicted. I'd smashed him to pieces in the ring so I would have mullured him out on the cobbles. I class myself as an all round better fighter out on the streets and not a bad one in the ring. I hope he learnt a valuable lesson that night. I was also moving direction but that was in my work life. I'd left the milk and was now a baggage handler at Heathrow Airport.

SALLY BLOOMFIELD

I first met Andy through my late husband, John, who was Andy's trainer. John would come home and talk about his boxers and Andy's name would crop up quite a bit. John said Andy was a bit of a rough diamond and was a bit like a wild horse which you had to steady because sometimes the rule book would go out of the window and he'd want to win at all costs. He'd bend the rules to win a fight. He lost a couple of fights from disqualification and he even bit one fella. I think he bit him on the ear or the shoulder. John would often tighten the reins with him. He was a tough nut but John was well pleased with him because he had all the potential to be a top class boxer.

When I first met him he was nothing like I expected. He was never rude to me or my two girls and in women's company he was a gentleman. He was always polite and always had a word for my girls. He never got above his station and in fact I can't ever recall him swearing in my or their company. He was always courteous to me but in the ring he turned into an animal. He feared no one and at times John had to educate him a bit and try to slow him down and get him to think what he was doing. He'd do anything to win. He was like a stone wall and no one could hurt him. He used to listen to John but a couple of times at the end of fights John had to jump in the ring to drag him back to his corner because Andy wanted to carry on after the bell. John used to F and blind at him but the respect was mutual. Andy, Rocky Kelly and Jeff Mcreish were all trained by John and he loved that style of fighter who gave their all.

I still see Andy and he recently spoke to me on the phone and I told him I'd found some pictures of him in a pinstriped suit and how handsome he used to look.

"What do you mean "used to look?" he said "I'm still handsome."

"Well, you're a bit on the large side now" I said.

"I'm not fat" he said.

"No, not much" I said, and we both laughed.

He thinks he's a bit of a Robbie Williams, a bit of a ladies' man. When he was married to Pauline he threw a party when he won one of the titles and he put on a lovely spread and I found him and her very sociable. They were a nice couple and over the years he's become a good friend to my family. When he retired from boxing he still kept in touch with John and at John's funeral we had a good chat about old times. I know if me and the girls ever needed him he'd be there for us. He's a lovely fella.

ROUND

A DREAM COME TRUE

MY JOB on the milk had gone tits up with the Dairy selling their rounds off in a move towards franchising everything. Being a milkman just wasn't the same. I knew a couple of mates that worked over the airport and they put a word in for me and I landed a job as a baggage handler with British Midland. My job was in a place called the Spur. It's where your bags go once you've checked in at the desks in the terminal. Once they've been weighed and tagged your bags go off on a conveyor belt which goes onto a shoot which sends the bags down to the area under the terminal and this area is known as the Spur. From there the bags are sorted into their flight numbers and are either loaded into metal bins or stacked loose on a baggage trolley. It's one fucking boring job. Its mind numbing. Most of the fellas there are Pakistani or Indian and after an hour I was bored shitless. If this was prison then the Spur was the punishment block, plus I was put on permanent earlies which meant me starting shift at 5.00 a.m, and working until about 2.00 p.m. when the late shift would come on duty and relieve us. The only thing was that I was free to do my boxing and my job didn't interfere with my training.

After the Collins fight I was still getting gyp with my elbow injury. I spoke to Harry and I decided to go to my local hospital and let them take a look at it. I ended up seeing a doctor who took a look at it and then explained that the waiting list to have the operation I needed on the National Health was over 6 months. He then told me that he ran a private clinic at another hospital and that it would cost £800 to have it done. It turned out I'd broken my elbow in two places. I had chips on the bone which were cutting into my padding which is called the burser, and it had become ulcerated. I was now in fucking agony with it and the doctor explained to me that once the operation had been done then I could be back in training within 2 weeks. I booked the op up and went into the hospital with £810 in cash in my trouser pocket, £600 was for the doctor carrying out the operation, £200, was for the anesthetist and the odd £10, was for phone calls and a bit of grub. When I came around from the operation some cunt had only taken the tenner out of my pocket, the thieving bastards. I ended up having to scrounge and borrow some change so that I could phone home. It could only happen to me.

Within a week I was back in the gym and 8 weeks after the operation I was in the ring with Wally Swift Junior defending my title. This was to be the second defence of my British title and the venue was The Royal Albert Hall, London. If I won this fight I got to keep the Lonsdale Belt, and I'd go down in the history books with the likes of Maurice Hope, Jimmy Batten, and Prince Rodney and Pat Thomas all good fighters in their time, and all outright winners of the belt. Wally was in a similar position as me, as he'd beaten Ensley Bingham to win the title, and like me had also beaten Tony Collins in a title fight. So he needed one more victory to win a Lonsdale Belt outright, so all this added a bit of spice to the fight. The fight was billed as ' The Close Encounter For, The Third Time.' Me and Wally by now knew one another inside out and it promised to be a great fight, the difference being that this time Wally would have two good hands and I'd have two good arms. I knew, I just knew, that in this fight I would knock Wally out. The way the last two fights had gone with him I knew it would only be a matter of time before I caught him right. In the previous two meetings with him Id hit him with some great shots and it was beyond belief how he'd stayed on his feet. I hit him with shots that would have knocked a Heavyweight out but Wally had stayed on his feet.

On the night of the fight the atmosphere was unbelievable and the Albert Hall is one special place to box at. As I made my way to the ring I've never had a feeling like it. Just being in that great arena gives you a lift. The whole place gives you a buzz and the reception Wally and me got was incredible and the fight was a near sell-out. The first bell goes and we meet in the centre of the ring and it's the same as the previous two fights between us as we start off toe to toe trading punches. We caught one another with some terrific shots and I don't know how I stayed on my feet at times, and likewise Wally. It must have been an exciting fight to watch.

In the second and third rounds it was much the same with the fight going one way and then the other. It was edge of the seat stuff. In the 4th I hit him with some of the best shots I've ever thrown. From the bell we met in the middle and I hit him, bang, bang, left, right, a straight jab and a right hand to the side of his head and I swear I could see his head spinning. I marched forward throwing big shots and the crowd was roaring me on. I hit him again and his legs wobbled and buckled. I hit him again and he nearly went. I had him. This was it. I was going to be the first man to knock Wally Swift out. I hit him again and again but he stayed on his feet. He'd never been down before and he'd never been stopped and he wasn't going to give that record up easily and he came back with a few shots of his own. His powers of recovery were out of this world. One second he was out on his feet, the next his head had cleared, his lungs full of fighting breath and he'd come firing back, but this time I wasn't going to let him off the hook. Harry and John were waving me on and I unloaded good shots smack into the middle of his face. He went backwards and I followed up with a left hook, a right hook and an upper cut and he was sparko on his feet. If the ropes hadn't of kept him upright and inside the ring he would have ended up in row 10, and you would have seen me standing in the ring on my own, and he would have been watching the fight with the spectators. He was gone as he leant on the ropes and all life had gone out of him. The fight in his eyes wasn't there. He stared blankly at me and for a split second I stopped. I looked at him and I didn't want to hurt him anymore. I had the utmost respect for him. He was like an old pal. He was finished and for a while I was frozen in time. I could hear the crowd roaring and shouting and screaming but I couldn't bring myself to hit him. He was defenceless. He was a beaten man. I was taking pity on him and if I had of hit him again I could quite possibly have hurt him for life. I could have put him in a coma. All these things went through my head and suddenly the ref came between us and stopped the fight. No sooner had the ref called a halt to it then Wally was back to his normal self but it was too late, the fight was over. I couldn't fucking believe it. One minute he was nearly down and out and within seconds he was complaining to the ref about him stopping the fight too early. He was one tough man who was clearly too brave for his own good. I just know that had I carried on hitting him he would have been seriously hurt. Even Wally Senior was complaining bitterly to the ref about stopping the fight. If he had of been my son my first concern would have been his safety. His health was more important than anything else wasn't it? I went over to Wally's corner and he was still complaining and remonstrating with the ref. "Don't be so fucking silly Wally," I said. "If I'd have hit you a couple more times you'd have ended up in a coma, you were fucking gone." He calmed down and I grabbed hold of him and gave him a cuddle and spun him around for the gathering paparazzi to get a few snaps. He wasn't a happy bunny and was well upset. I wish I could put the video of that fight in this book. It was a classic. I gave him punishment for 3 and a bit rounds and likewise he gave me punishment for 3 and a bit rounds. It was unbelievable.

I was now the proud owner of a Lonsdale Belt. I'd dreamt of this moment since I was 12 years old. The belt was wrapped around my waist and a magnum bottle of champagne was popped open in my changing room. I didn't shake it over people Grand Prix style but instead drank most of it. It was too expensive to waste. I'm a tight arse anyway so why waste it? Gary Mason, the ex heavyweight boxer, was a pundit working that night for T.V. ringside. He had been commentating on my last fight with Wally and had stated that if it wasn't for Wally breaking his hand then he believed that Wally would have won that fight. Now I've got it into my head that now the fights finished then I've got to go and see Mason and tell him how wrong he was, about that last fight. I showered and got changed and went in search of him. Someone pointed out that he was working in the T.V. gantry which was set high up on top of a scaffolding tower. I climbed up the outside of the tower and popped my head up between Gary Norman the other main pundit and Mason. Gary Norman was a true pro and carried on talking as I appeared, he sees me, pop up "Andy this is live T.V. so no swearing please." The thing was I'd drunk so much champagne on an empty stomach that the bubbly had gone to my head and I was feeling half pissed. "No, no," I said, "I just want to say what a great fight it was and I would also like to put Gary straight about me and Wally's last fight." "Gary," I said, "all you kept on about was Wally Swift's broken hand but no-one knew that I'd boxed with an elbow broken in two places and if I wasn't injured that night then I would have done to him then what I done to him tonight." He couldn't really say a lot and just shrugged his shoulders and said "whooaaa." And tried to laugh it off. He knew he was wrong.

In a T.V. interview straight after the fight I told them it was my boyhood dream to win a Lonsdale Belt outright. But the bloke doing the interview then said that in his opinion it was the first time in my three meetings with Wally that I'd wobbled him with a shot. I managed to control my emotions and behave in a proper manner, but I knew inside I was shaking with anger and rage. What I would have loved to have said live on T.V. was "You're having a fucking laugh, I've wobbled him in every fight we've had and I've nearly stopped him in every fight but he kept on coming back. It was like switching a light on and off."

After a few days off I was back at work over at the airport and I took in my newly won belt to show everyone. One of the managers, who was a bit of a flash cunt, fancied having a bit of a spar with me and if the truth was known he fancied himself as a bit of a fighter. I went into his office and he shut the door behind us and pulled out a pair of gloves and put them on and he shaped up to me. "You sure about this?" I asked. "Yeah," he said, bouncing up and down. "Let's see what you're made of," he snarled as he tucked his chin into his chest and danced around me prodding out his jab. I moved in close and with one smooth movement sent a hook crashing into his body just below his ribs. He fell crumbled into a heap on the floor and writhed about in agony trying to catch his breath. He laid there like a sack of shit. I took the gloves off; he had handed me and pulled open the blinds. Loads of black, brown and white faces were squashed up against the glass trying to see what had gone on. The next day I was put back on a rota where I had to do both early and days, and late shifts. My permanent early shifts were a thing of the past. This bloke later turned out to be a right wrong 'un who would stab anyone in the back to get on. He thought he was one of the lads who'd come from the streets and had done well for himself, but in the end all his arse licking and groveling around the airport managers, and his golf days out, counted for nothing. He was like the rest of us, disposable and replaceable as he turned out to be a right fucking grass.

JOE SMITH
Professional golfer, bare knuckle fighter and boxing and music promoter

I first met Andy in 92/93 when I walked straight off the street and into his gym. It was the nearest pro gym to where I was living at the time and I just wanted to learn from the best. I was 20 years old and was as keen as fuck.

I'd gone over to Harry's gym in the car with my cousin, Jimmy Stokin, who is known to be a bit of a fighter himself. All the way there Jim was drumming it into me not to make a cunt of myself. Jim had been drinking with Johnnie Bloomfield who told Jim to bring me over if I was brave enough to spar with his British champion. As we walked in through the doors Jim again told me not to act like a cunt and liven meself up and shape up. I assured him I wouldn't let myself or him down.

"Don't embarrass me" said Jim.

I got changed and was put in the ring with a fella named Tony who Johnnie Bloomfield said was about to have his first pro fight at Heavyweight. We started off the sparing session with me hurtling out of my corner and straight into him I had Jimmy's words of wisdom still in my head. Bang, Bang, I crashed shots into this Tony's head and put him down.

"Whoa whoa," people were shouting at ringside.

"Stop, stop for fucks sake you've nearly taken the man's head off."

I came out the blocks at 100 mph. I looked at Jim and his eyes lift to the heavens as he shrugged his shoulders.

"Joe, for fucks sake calm down, it's only a sparring session."

"Fuck me Jim," I'm thinking "make ya fucking mind up."

I then calmed down and we had a leisurely spar. Andy then got in with this Tony fella wearing what I can only describe as a sort of Hannibal Lectar mask. It was a re-inforced head guard with metal bars on it. He'd suffered a serious nose injury in a previous sparring session and he looked mean in it but he was mean anyway because it wasn't long before he put poor Tony down on the canvas with a barrage of punches and Tony was his good mate. What did he do to people he didn't know, like me?

Me and Andy got in with one another and he came straight across the ring at me. Crash, crash, crash, he fired shots into me. He was fit, ready and above all, useful. How I stayed on my feet I'll never know. I've got a big heart and can take a punch and there was no way that I'd go down. He continued to throw big shots at me and at times he hurt me. He pushed me to the limits but slowly I steadied myself and caught him with some half-decent shots of my own. It turned out I was good practice for him.

He'd switch from head to body, body to head. It was good practice for him, and he looked like he was enjoying himself. My chin stood up to his assaults and over the course of a few weeks I increased my fitness, and confidence. In the end we sparred for months together. I used to call him 'The Mental Milkman' I remember hearing the tale of him sparing with Joe Bugner Jnr and apparently Andy nearly broke him clean in half with one of his body shots. I was on an evening out once with a few of the old pros and me and Glen Mcrory, Mike Tyson's old sparing partner and now TV pundit, were talking about Andy. 'You wouldn't want to try to pinch his milk round takings, would you?' joked Glen. Andy has got so much respect from fellow pros, I've been to boxing shows and dinners where they have a charity auction of gloves and photos and things with an MC in the middle of the ring shouting out who's bidding and who's paying what for what, when it comes to the buyer of a certain item being a bit slow in getting his money out then I've heard certain MCs, shout ' If you don't hurry up and get your money out, I'll send Andy Till over'

I trained with him leading up towards his fights with Wally Swift and Tony Collins. When he fought Collins Andy was right on top of his game. He was probably the best and strongest Light Middleweight in the world. He was at his peak. It was a man against a boy when he fought Collins. Me cousin, Jimmy, had quite a bit of money on Andy to win and a few travelers question Jimmy's loyalty towards another traveler. Jim told them he wasn't backing against another traveler; but was backing what he fancied. He told people he'd seen me, who was no fool, spar with Andy and in his view Andy would be too strong and too good for Collins.

"I'd congratulate Tony Collins if he was to beat Andy Till but I'll tell you he's as strong as an ox and I can't see him getting beat" he said, and as it turns out Jim was right. Les Stevens, Collins's trainer, couldn't believe just how strong and up for it Andy was. Collins had wound Andy up before the fight but none of us knew that. Andy had kept it to himself.

I never got a tanner or even a half a pence for sparring with Andy. Some of his sparring partners were on £60 to £100 a session. I got fuck all, not even a ticket for any of the two fights, in which I helped him prepare. In the end it wasn't about money, it was about me learning a trade and to be honest it was a tough way to learn but I learnt just how good Andy was.

Since we met we've become good friends. We've been to Spain on holiday and we've done business together. Me, Andy and my brother, John, were on my debt collecting team together. We went down to Wales to collect £102 thousand pounds from a golf club. The geezer that run it was from London and when we first approached him he was acting rather cocky.

"I owe no one fuck all" he smirked.

We were all dressed in black leather jackets and we had the gangster look about us. We looked the part and as we talked he made out that he was reaching for something under his desk.

"I wouldn't be silly" I told him, "we could carry on this conversation at your home address," and I told him exactly where he lived. He shit himself. He wasn't so cocky now. We stuck to him like shit to a blanket. Where he walked around that room we followed. We didn't give him an inch. In the end I think my good looks and Andy's charm shone through and we walked out with the money.

We've had a couple of little fall outs but its all about respect and we remain good mates. Andy normally gets his way but on a couple of occasions we've called our minor disagreements draws. When we see one another we hug and shake hands and have total respect for one another. People often ask me how I think Andy would have got on in the bare knuckle fighting world, my cousin Jimmy and his brother Wally were to me legends, Jim versus Andy on the cobbles would have been a classic on par with an Ali v Frazier or an Ali v Foreman. Andy would have made a great knuckle fighter, one of the best that's for sure.

These days I'm doing a bit of music and boxing promoting and trying to get back into the golf. I'm still ambitious when it comes to the golf and I had my best season last year so look out Tiger, Gypsy Joe's on ya case!

ROUND

10

MOVING UP IN CLASS

THINGS were going well for me in the ring but my home life was in a bit of a mess. Me and Pauline seemed to be at each others throats constantly. A lot of the rows were about our finances, or the lack of them that is. As soon as money came in on one hand it was paid out with the other and like a lot of families we were finding that at times making ends meet was a struggle. I had my airport job, plus money from my boxing and Pauline was working as the manageress of a leisure centre but like most women, she knew how to spend a few quid. She was also away a lot doing courses for the job so I was working, training and looking after the kids and the house. I was fucking worn out. Did she really have to be out of the house so much? She was never happy with what she had. We were still having our family holidays abroad but when we'd get back from Spain or somewhere the bills would quickly mount up. It was an uphill battle to make ends meet.

Before the last Wally Swift fight Harry had been looking into getting me a World Title shot. There were four world champions at that time, which were the IBF, title holder, Italian Gianfranco Rossi, who seemed he would never box outside of Italy, John David Jackson, who was the WBO champion, who had beaten my old mate Chris Pyatt. I remember Chris saying after his fight with Jackson, what an awkward southpaw style Jackson had. 'Terrible Terry Harris, held the WBC belt and the big punching, Argentinean,

Julio Caesar Vasquez held the WBA belt. Harry and I say this with no disrespect, was not as financially equipped as the big time promoters in the world scene, and he struggled to get his foot in the door, with the big boys. He was no Don King or Mickey Duff. I remember Harry telling me at the time that Rossi would want something like £375 thousand, to fight me and Jackson would want near on half a million pounds to fight me in the States. However, Harry just didn't have that sort of dough. Them prices was well out of his league so we went down the ladder and set our sights at a shot at the European title which was held by France's Laurent Boudouani. He had an impressive record of 23 wins and 1 loss so he was no mug. John rushed around trying to find video tapes of him for me to study but I told him not to bother. I'd never watched a tape of an opponent and I wasn't going to start now.

My training for the fight wasn't going too well as I'd moved out of the marital bed and was sleeping downstairs on the settee, not the best preparation for a big fight. It got that bad I was doing my own cooking, washing and ironing. The situation at home had got to this and my head was in a spin. I just couldn't think straight. Only a couple of real close pals at work really knew what I was going through. One main thing in my favour was Boudouani had never fought outside of France. He was a banger but had never gone beyond 6 rounds in his first fifteen fights. I'd done the full 12 rounds a few times so I knew I had the staying power. If I could get him over the half way mark and, as always, come on stronger in the latter rounds, then I knew I'd half a chance of winning. Boudouani was 26 years old and came from Sallanches in France and had been a pro since April 1987. My fight with him would be the second defence of his European crown. Out of his 23 pro fights, he'd stopped 21 of those opponents inside the distance. He'd only been taken the distance once with a point's win against Anthony Ivory. His only defeat to date was against the world class American, Gilbert Baptist, who in turn had gone the distance, twice with WBC champion Terry Norris. Who in a lot of people's books was the best pound for pound fighter in the world at the time? Boudouani's older brother Robert, was a useful Super- Middleweight on the French domestic scene a few years back.

Some mornings I was getting up at 3.00 a.m. to go to work but I never really let on to Harry and John that mentally and physically I wasn't right, at times I was drained, but there was no way I'd pull out of the fight. That wasn't me. I'd been given the opportunity to fight for the European crown so this was my big chance. I believed I would come out on top in the fight no matter what life had thrown at me. I had so much self- belief. As I said his one defeat had been at the hands of the world class American, Gilbert Baptist, who halted Boudouani in 8 rounds. He'd won the title in November '92 from his fellow countryman, Jean Fontana in 3 rounds. Fontana had beaten my old mate, Wally Swift, in a previous title fight. In Boudouani's first defence of his crown he knocked out Ramalo Casamonica in 9 rounds of vicious punching. He'd stopped 21 of his opponents inside the distance so as I say, he had quite an impressive record. Was I bothered? Was I fuck? Harry had done well to get this geezer over here and had got together with Lennox Lewis's promoter and manager, Frank Maloney, to put the show on. It was to be held on the 23rd of June at The Picketts Lock Centre, Edmonton, North London, and the tickets went like hot cakes.

On the day of the fight my weight was spot on. When I left my house I was dead on the weight at 10st. 13lbs. My weight was perfect, at least something was making me happy. I'd not eaten or drunk anything that day, I'd had a couple of pisses and after a good night's kip on the settee I was brand new. I got to the 'Thomas A Beckett' gym down at the Old Kent Road where the arranged pre-fight weigh in was being held. Everyone gathered around as I stepped onto the official scales but the scales had been placed on wooden floor boards and where everyone was watching and leaning forward and moving closer to see them, the needle on the scales moved as well. My weight as the needle on the scales moved and bounced around went from 11 stone and 2 lb to 10st 13lb but the officials called my weight out as 11st and 1/4lb so to make the weight for the fight I had to lose nearly 2lb. "No trouble," I'm thinking, so I went away, put my tracksuit on and a black plastic bin liner over the top to make me sweat, and skipped in the gym for a while. I then dried myself off with a towel, stripped off to me pants and stepped back on the scales. The crowds gathered around, again the needle jiggles about and they call my weight as 11stone and 1/2 lb. I'd just sweated my bollocks off and had come back heavier. How the fuck had that happened? The Boudouani team disagreed with our claims that it was the floor not being level and that it was giving me an inaccurate weight reading, so I had to put my gear back on and went out and done a 3 mile run. By the time I'd got back the place was nearly empty as people had now lost interest and had drifted off. I got back on the scales and weighed in at 10st 13lb. Now I was passed feeling hungry and didn't want to feed myself up with grub or liquids in case I got hit with one up the guts in the ring and threw up. We headed over to the venue and got ready. As I left the dressing room and made my way to the ring the atmosphere was electric. The place was choc-a-block and they were hanging from the rafters.

The first bell went and the crowd roared me on. We met in the middle of the ring and bang, bang I let my first flurry of shots go into his head. He fired back and we felt one another out for the rest of the round as it ends even Stevens. In the second round he catches me with a terrific right cross and over I go. I got up and came back with a right upper cut, a left hook and a right hand that wobbles him. He instinctly grabs hold of me, hangs on and won't let go and I know I've hurt him. The ref from Denmark tells us to break and then warns me, not him, about holding. We come out for the third and the crowd is still booing the ref for warning me about holding. I catch him almost straight away with a left hook and his legs buckled. I move forward and throw another left hook that misses him completely and I fall to the floor. The lack of sleep, food and liquid and the earlier running and skipping have taken its toll.

Boudouani hadn't touched me. I'd gone down exhausted and under my own lack of steam but the ref, to everyone's surprise, gives me a standing eight count. More screams and boos from the crowd and shouts of "cheat, cheat cheat" ring out. I've now lost two of the three rounds. The bell goes to end the round and I sit down in my corner. I feel drained but in my mind I know that in all of my fights I've come on stronger in the latter rounds. My own pep talk inside my head spurs me on and I come out for the fourth picking him off with good crisp shots, with a spring in my step. I'm sharper now and I'm catching him with some good shots. I hit him with a good combination. He goes back stumbling across the ropes and he then uses the ropes to catapult himself forward and looks at me before head-butting me above my right eye. It was the most deliberate butt you've ever seen. It was so blatant. "You cunt," I shouted, and the ref ignored me and called for us to box on. He didn't even look at me as a gash opened up above and below my eye, which straight away is pissing out blood. I was still catching him but the blood was pouring into my eye, and obscuring my vision. The bell went and I went back to my corner and told Harry I was fucked and my eye was knackered. I was emotionally and physically drained. Boudouani sat in his corner and his people quickly toweled off the blood from his forehead where he'd caught me, deliberately with his head. I tell Harry I can't carry on, the ref comes over and that's the end of the fight. I put it down to a bad day at the office.

Before the fight Pauline had come into the changing rooms to speak to me. I thought she'd come in to tell me I'd forgotten to hoover or dust before I'd left for the fight, but her coming in only fucked my head up even more. She came in after the fight but never really said a lot. It was all too much for me. I think I got about 25 grand for that fight so she might have thought I was in a good mood and loaded and she could get a new dress or a pair of shoes out of me. It wasn't my best pay day nor was it one of my better performances. I still had my British Light Middleweight crown but I was down for weeks after that fight. I ended up having 27 stitches in that cut eye but my pride was more dented and bruised than my face. Harry and John knew that I was disappointed but it never came into my head to turn the game in. I wanted to carry on and felt I had a lot left to offer. There was nothing in the contract for a re-match but to tell you the truth I wasn't that bothered. I could concentrate on the domestic scene and there was nothing stopping me from coming again and challenging for the European Title or even a World Title if I put in some decent performances. Stranger things had happened in the boxing world.

I did hear, and whether it's true or not I don't know, but Boudouani fought again 6 weeks after our fight and was knocked out by his opponent and put in a coma for a week. It then goes that a year later he was back fighting and won the World Title. That I just can't believe because normally if you were put in a coma your career would be over, you're finished. But as I say, with all the politics and power struggles in boxing anything is possible. Fiction is stranger than the truth in the noble art.

ALAN GADD
AIRPORT WORKER

I first met Andy about 1993. I was working as a loader for British Midland and he walked into the crew room one day. My first impressions of him was "fuck me, he looks evil, don't have a go at him," but when you get to know him he's a nice fella with a heart of gold, but raving fucking mad.

I went to see him fight Robert McCraken at Watford Town Hall. At work he was a pain in the arse and the first words out of his mouth at 5 a.m. in the morning was

"What time do you reckon we'll be away today?"

He was a joy to work with and made the day go quick He was liked by everyone. Anyone with food was Andy's friend. He was like a hungry dog. He'd ponce food off of anyone. He loved the curry's what the Indian boys would bring in. He was liked by everyone there. He was a piss taker. When he first started he'd be up for doing anything. One day we were unloading sides of frozen horse meat and it would take two of us just to lift it out of the hold of the plane and onto the back of the truck. Andy was throwing them the length of the hold on his own. He was as strong as an ox, but as he got bigger with all the crisps, chocolate, biscuits and curry, he got lazier. In the end it was a job to get him to move. He didn't want to unload or load by hand, he just wanted to drive the machinery. That's why he got fat. Plus he used to think he was a good looking Casanova. He thought all the air hostesses fancied him. He was as vain as fuck. We had another pro boxer working with us at the time who we all used to joke had adverts on the bottom of his boxing boots because he got knocked out so often. Andy was once asked by one of the Indian lads who would win if him and the other boxer Tony Velinor ever met in the ring. Andy looked at him menacingly.

"Put it this way, it would be the end of his career."

Before Andy had got there Tony had been telling everyone what a fantastic boxer he was. He had to shut his mouth when Andy got there because a fantastic boxer had arrived. He was a card, so funny.

I remember me and another loader Ted Worral were sitting in an electric tug waiting for a flight to come in at 4 in the morning and Andy was on the job. He was too lazy to go and find another tug so he thought it would be funny to pull Ted out of the driving seat and nick our tug. Ted's foot slipped off the brake and hit the accelerator. The front of the tug hit Andy on the leg and knocked him to the ground. It ran up his leg and over him as he lay there. He had tyre marks from his ankle to his thigh but still got up, laughed and carried on working. We thought he was dead. We only heard him moaning and he sounded like Blakey off of On The Buses. Ted went as white as a sheet but I sat there laughing my bollocks off.

I'm now driving a black cab in London and since leaving the airport have bumped into Andy a couple of times and he's still as nutty as fuck.

ROUND

Me, John and Harry ready for lift off.

Me and my son, luke, aged 9 with John and Harry at The Albert Hall.

Me with the Lonsdale and WBC Belts.

Me and 'Mad Frankie Fraser', who's the nuttier?

'Sorry you're not on the list, so you can't come in'..

What can I say?

This man was the light heavyweight champion of Tenerife and he fancied his chances in the ring with me. He learnt the hard way!

Me and my brother John.

Me and Harry Holland who's now an actor in his own right after showing his acting skills in the soap East Enders.

Me and Martin King who helped me write the book.

Me and step-son Tom, he's a lovely lad.

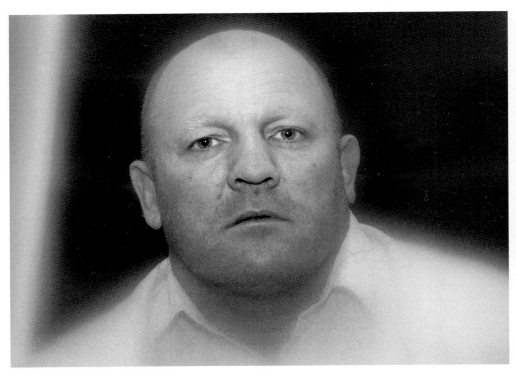

Penny for my thoughts.

'Right Harry, you owe me money

Pat Wilson and me at the NortholtBoxing Cub.

The showers still don't work.

You never lose it. I think I'll make a come back. Me at my old amateur gym.

'Help, help'. Someone help me i can't move!

Pat Wilson who's played a huge part in my life. A nicer fella you couldn't wish to meet. Pat was more like a father to me than my own dad.

Here's one for the girls. Me now, I think I look rather attractive in this shot. I don't think boxing has altered my boyish, film star looks, do you?

THE ZULUS

I T SEEMED my marriage was over but my boxing career certainly wasn't. I was out of the ring for 8 months after my failed European challenge but was still dedicated and training hard at the gym. I saw that defeat as just a bad day at the office. The way I looked at it was if I hadn't of been nutted and cut then I believe I would have finished it after 7 or 8 rounds.

My next opponent was Birmingham's Robert McCracken, who'd had 18 fights and 18 wins so I knew he wasn't half bad. The fight was held on the 23rd February '94 at Watford Town Hall and well over half of the audience was made up of Birmingham City's infamous football hooligans, The Zulus. A nicer group of chaps you couldn't wish to meet.

The first bell went and almost immediately McCraken went on the defensive. He held his guard high and jabbed and moved and that seemed to be his game plan. I fought in my usual way and came forward looking to unload, but as soon as I'd plant my feet to tee off a shot he'd jab and move. The bout went on like this for almost the entire fight and what didn't help was the crowd trouble. While me and McCraken were fighting in the ring sections of the crowd were also, knocking lumps out of each other. There were outbreaks of violence all over the arena and one time the police even came into the hall to try quell the violence. These weren't boxing fans, these were football fans watching a boxing match and not knowing how to behave. Supposedly McCraken's brother was one of the main faces in the Birmingham Zulu mob. Because of the trouble outside the ring the ref stopped the fight twice. The M.C. announced from the ring that if there was any more trouble then the fight would not carry on. I was well aware of the bother going on but I had other things on my mind. I felt good for this fight much better mentally than I did for the Boudouani fight but all McCraken did was either jab and run or hold on and tie me up, or get on his bike and keep away from me. He didn't hurt me once and to tell you the truth Wally Swift and W.O. Wilson hurt me more than McCraken, but he had a game plan and he stuck to it.

At the end of the fight I honestly thought that I'd won, comfortably, but in the end he beat me by half a point. Technically he was a good boxer but he had no power. I think the crowd played a big part in him getting the decision. He later went over to America to box but never really done anything over there. Almost everywhere he boxed there was crowd trouble. I later saw him, at one of Audley Harrison's early fights. Audley had trained at the Northolt gym as an amateur and he's a right nice fella. At the Harrison fight he was soing some commentary work for T.V. and now he's a trainer and I think he trains his son who's now a pro boxer. He's also got Howard Eastman in his stable. Anyway, he's sitting at ring side and as I walk past he calls out to me.

"All right Andy?".

"Not really," I reply as I walk back towards him.

"Why, what's up," he asks.

"You know as well as I know that you never won that fight we had."

"It weren't my fault," he replied, and I took that as a way of him admitting he knew that he'd never won that fight. For him to say that it weren't his fault says it all in my book. His win, his victory and my defeat was all boxing politics. Robert McCraken was Micky Duff's golden boy. How would the crowd of reacted if I'd have won. I'd have had to have knocked him out to get a draw. He never won that fight, the crowd won that fight for him. A mate of mine who'd never ever been to see me fight bought a ticket and never even made it to the arena. He was in a pub near to the town hall and was in the toilet when a bloke came up to him and asked him if he was there for the boxing. He tells the man that he was there to see me box and the fella pulls out a blade and slashes him down the face and he later had 14 stitches put in the wound and never even sees the fight. That was just one of the many horror stories I've heard from that night. What had that sort of incident got to do with boxing?

I was now 31 years of age and after that fight I called it a day and retired from boxing. I stayed at my job over at the airport but I began to pile on the weight. It wasn't really hard graft although when you did work it was hard for maybe an hour or so and then it was back into the crew room for a coffee and another Mars bar or packet of crisps and then over to the canteen for a curry or egg and chips. It was all junk food. Also I'd stopped going to the gym to train. My weight and waist seemed to be spiralling out of control. My best friend had become the crew room vending machine, plus I had a little scam with it. Instead of putting in coins and getting something to eat out of it I'd tip it on its side or give it a shake and whatever fell out the flap on the front was mine. Harry and John never once tried to persuade me not to give up the boxing. I think they knew the personal problems I was going through. At home my marriage came to a complete end and finished when I ended up getting nicked and having an injunction served on me to keep away from my marital home.

One particular day me and her were rowing and it went on nearly all day. She lost her temper and punched me and then calmed down. Then we rowed again, she flared up again and scratched and kicked me and then she went calm again. Later she started again and tried to bite me. I tried to hold her off and talk to her and she punched me in the stomach and tried to bring her knee up into my bollocks as I was holding her wrists to prevent her from hitting me. It went on and on for hours and in the end I could do and say no more to stop her. I grabbed my coat and headed for the front door but as I pulled it open she came up behind me and kicked it shut, nearly taking my fingers off in the process.

"For fucks sake, can't you leave me alone," I shouted at her. "If I ever was to hit ya I'd fucking hurt you," I then lost my patience completely and I'm not to proud to say I was disgusted with my reaction but there's only so much a man can take, so with that I punched her on her leg and grabbed her by the throat. I quickly let go and with that I pulled open the front door and left her lying there with her mouth wide open. I went straight down to the Old Bill station and spoke to the copper behind the desk. I told him the outline of the story and he asked me my name and address and i said could they go down to my house and have a word with her before the whole thing got out of hand.

"Do you live at 32 Grosvenor Avenue Mr. Till," the copper asked me.

"Yes," I replied.

"You're under arrest" he said, and with that came my side of the counter and arrested me.

She'd beat me to it and had already phoned the police and reported me. I had three scratch marks down my face, a bite mark on my bottom lip, a bite mark on my eyebrow and one on my body and head where she'd whacked me with her shoes. I went to court and that's when the injunction was served on me. I wasn't allowed within two hundred yards of my own house. British justice at its best? After about 3 months I was allowed back by her to go and pick my clothes and personal belongings up but as I was leaving with black bin liners full of clobber she threw a big bunch of keys at me which hit me straight on the back of my head and fuck me did it hurt? I felt blood trickling down my neck and onto the clean white shirt I had on. The back of my head was stinging and throbbing with pain. I looked around at her as I stopped just outside the front door, still keeping a grip on the gear I had balancing under my arms and in my hands.

"What did you do that for?" I asked, and shook my head in disgust. I began walking up the path away from her and CRASH the same bunch of keys hit me in the back of the head again. I dropped all my belongings and grabbed hold of her by the back of the neck. Across the road from the house an old lady had been cleaning her front windows and had seen everything.

"Here love," I said "you're my witness and you've just seen what this nutter's just done to me." By now the whole of my shirt was covered in blood and it felt like the blood was trickling out of hundreds of little puncture marks caused by the keys she'd thrown at me. I threw my gear into the car and drove straight down to the police station where the original incident had been reported and by a chance in a million the same horrible copper who had arrested me was on duty behind the desk. He looked up at me as I walked in with dried blood on my face, back of my head and neck.

"Can I help you Sir?" he asked.

"Yes officer I'd like to report my wife for attacking me less than an hour ago with a heavy set of metal keys."

He looked me up and down and said "I'm sorry Sir but we don't settle domestic disputes here."

As I said before, British justice at its best?

After being forced out of my house I moved in with a friend of a friend who offered me a spare room in his three bedroomed house and I in turn helped him decorate it. I suppose my last resort for somewhere to live would have been back at my mum and dads but as time went on I saw less and less of them. Even my own children hadn't had a lot to do with them. I suppose in their own funny way they loved all their grandchildren but they just didn't have a clue how to treat kids. I used to take the children around there to visit them, and I'd told them all about my own upbringing and how me and all my brothers and sisters had been treated badly, so I hid nothing from them. I remember once I was round their house with my son, Luke, who had just started standing and walking a few steps. He was still not steady on his feet so he'd use the furniture to help himself balance. Me mum and dad were both heavy smokers so being the lazy, dirty bastards they were there'd always be a full ashtray on the coffee table. Luke was pottering about and having fun and somehow knocked the ashtray off the table and onto the floor. The old man jumped up and went to clip him around the ear.

" Oi what are you doing?" I shouted, and he stopped dead in his tracks.

"Well, he's knocked the ashtray over and he's got to learn" said the old man.

"He's 9 months old and he don't know he's done it" I said.

"Well tell him," said the old man, pointing at little Luke as he sat back down in his threadbare armchair.

"Listen," I said "I don't want my son growing up thinking the same as I think of you."

"What do you mean by that?" he asked.

"Well, if I have to explain it to you then you must be brain dead" I replied.

I knew he didn't like what I'd said to him and I knew he'd taken offence to it but that's how thick skinned, my mum and dad were. There was never any toys there for me or my brothers or sisters' kids to play with. They never really made the children that welcome or made a fuss of them. They never played the doting grandparents that's for sure.

After a while I moved out of me mate Rory's house and moved in with a girl I knew from years ago. To this day I don't know why I ever got involved with her as she was a raving nutcase. She'd been after me for years and I should have seen the warning signs but my main brain in my trousers took over. Anyway, I ended up moving in with her but the thing was she was pregnant with someone else's baby. We ended up staying together for a few years, but it wasn't the happiest period of my life. It just shows that care in the community doesn't work so lock up your rabbits, there's a bunny boiler on the loose.

Around this time I had a yearning to get back in the ring. I'd started jogging again and was on a bit of a keep fit regime. I didn't want to be a fat bastard no more. In the pro game there'd been a few cases of boxers sustaining serious injuries whilst in the ring. Michael Watson, Gerald Mcleland, Bradley Stone had all suffered serious head injuries and had lapsed into comas. Spencer Oliver was another one, so the boxing game wasn't getting the best of publicity and there were even calls to outlaw the sport from certain quarters. Anyway I was back down the gym and got back into shape, or some sort of shape. I needed the money badly so Harry fixed me up a fight at Super Middleweight against Darren Griffiths who'd had 23 fights. I'd not been in the ring for over 18 months and here I was at the York Hall, Bethnal Green, making my comeback. I think I got about 8 grand for the fight, which to me wasn't half bad money.

During my break from the ring I'd even got the taste for the booze and would go out with my mates and sometimes get well pissed. I never took drugs but once some cunt slipped an ecstasy tablet in my drink and it knocked me bandy. I'd originally got my weight down to Middleweight and the original plan was to fight Gary Stretch who'd moved up a weight. He was now the British Light Middleweight champion and challenged Chris Eubank for his world title belt. Anyway, I ended up instead in the ring with Darren Griffiths from Wales. Looking at it now it was the wrong move. The first few rounds I felt good and it felt like I'd never been away but then he caught me with a shot and put me on my arse. I wasn't hurt but to my surprise the ref stopped the fight. As I say I wasn't hurt or in trouble, I was more off balance when he caught me, but because of all the publicity surrounding the recent injuries in the ring boxing referee's seemed all too keen to call a halt to proceedings for the slightest of things. Gone were the days it seemed of 12 round, toe to toe wars, they were a thing of the past. I looked at the ref when he stopped the fight.

"What do you mean you're stopping the fucking fight?" I growled at him through my gum shield.

He never even gave me a count. I was up at three with a clear head. I was disgusted with the decision and swore blind I'd never step into a boxing ring again. I was as sick as a pig. I was gutted but I've stuck to my word. Darren Griffiths went on to do as expected, fuck all. Beating me was the highlight of his career.

CAROL (Girlfriend)

I met Andy in Oscar's nightclub about 11 years ago and my first impression was how arrogant he was. He was horrible, I didn't like him. He was so full of himself. He was having a great time on the dance floor all on his own. Lots of people seemed to know him. My sister had once been engaged to Andy's mate who Andy had been staying with when his marriage broke up. He came over to me and shook my hand and asked if I knew who he was. I said "no, and I don't want to either." I think he introduced himself as "Andy Till, boxer, 3 times British champion, buy us a drink." His mate actually bought us a drink and I think my sister even cheekily pocketed the change.

We became friends for a long time after that and I helped him get through a bad patch in his life. My impressions of him have changed and the real Andy Till is a lovely man. I love him to bits. He makes out he's arrogant but that's all an act. He's good to my family and most of the time he's a joy to be with. I hope one day we end up getting married and at long last he's seen who his real friends are. Most of the hangers on have now gone and so now he can just be himself.

ROUND

12

SECONDS OUT, THE 12th AND FINAL ROUND

S O THAT was it and that was me retired. I'd had 24 pro fights, won 19 (9 kos) and lost 5. Not a bad record? That was it. That was me retired for good. There was no coming back but to be truthful I did toy with the idea of having a bash at the unlicensed game. But the money wasn't really there, plus no one wanted to fight me. I've been to few of them unlicensed shows and when I've been at ringside I've wanted to get up there, but I wouldn't belittle myself. I did get the buzz sitting there watching, but trouble in my life, in one shape or another and fighting never seemed to be far away from me.

One day I was driving to work over at the airport and a geezer cut me up in his car. It was on the Hayes By-Pass near Western International market. He pulled across sharply in front of me, causing me to swerve and brake suddenly, so I flashed me lights and beeped him. He slowed right down and slammed his brakes on and I nearly smashed into the back of him. He then accelerated and roared away. The thing is he never got that far away from me as he got caught at the next set of traffic lights so I pulled up behind him, got out of the car and went to speak to him. His window was half open and I told him he was driving like a fucking idiot and that one day he'd end up hurting someone and that he was nothing but a prick. He never said a word so I walked back to my car, happier I'd caught him and had given him a sound bit of advice. I back got inside the car and pulled my seat belt on. As I looked up and turned the keys in the ignition I could see him coming towards me. He was suited and booted like a businessman, but in his hand he was carrying what looked like a long screwdriver. My first reaction was "fuck me he's going to stab me." I quickly undid the seat belt and opened the car door but as I was halfway out and slightly crouched over he stabbed me in the arm. I stood up fully and turned to face him and he swung his arm around and stabbed me in the back. I came straight over the top of the arm he'd used to stab me with a right hand, and knocked him spark out. He was a tall lump, about 6ft 2" and looked like an Arab type. As he lay there having a kip I phoned the police on my mobile and explained the situation to them. Motorists were slowing down to take a look but not one person stopped to ask if I needed help or ask if I was O.K. The knife wounds I had wasn't really hurting but that was probably because of my adrenalin pumping, and there wasn't that much blood. It seemed ages since I'd made the call to the old bill and there was no sign of them if I'd have had no tax on me motor or a bald tyre, then I'm sure there would have been one of them around. I phoned the police again, and told them that I'd been stabbed in a road rage incident and that the fella had been knocked out but was starting to come round. As he woke up and tried to get to his feet I cut the police off the line, put the phone back in my pocket and hit him again. The thing was he still had the screwdriver in his hand and I was taking no chances so I flopped him again. I was back on the phone to the Old Bill.

"How long are you going to be?" I asked, "because if he wakes up again I'm going to do him good and proper."

"We will be two minutes, stay calm," was their reply.

I put the phone back in my pocket and straight away the cunt was trying to get back onto his feet again. I couldn't have hit him hard enough. So I've hit him again and down he went and this time for good measure I put the boot into his ribs a couple of times.

"Stay down there you cunt" I growled at him.

The police and two ambulances turn up but there's no sign of the screwdriver he's used to stab me. He's put in one ambulance and I'm put in another but we turn up at the same hospital at the same time. It was like a fucking 'Carry On film'! We were both wheeled into a waiting area on separate trolleys and me and this geezer I've just had the fight with are no more than four feet apart as we lay on stretchers waiting to be seen by a nurse or doctor. I get on my phone and tell the Old Bill about the situation and how the geezer who's just tried to kill me is laying less than four feet away from me.

"Mr. Till" said the copper, "are you using your mobile phone to make this call from the hospital?"

"Yes" I replied.

"Well I suggest," said the copper, "you end this call because you can be arrested and charged for the misuse of a mobile phone inside a hospital."

"What"

The thing was the bloke wasn't threatening me or giving me any lip. He couldn't, because he couldn't even talk. I'd broken his cheek-bone and jaw and put a gash down the side of his nose and had broken three of his ribs. He was hardly in any state to get tricky with me. He just sat there looking at me like John Merrick the Elephant man but I knew this cunt could be dangerous if he could lay his hands on a knife or something sharp or pointed. I'd never been in a situation like this before and the lucky thing was, or unlucky for him, was that I knew how to punch, and defend myself. I'd been training long enough as a boxer and good job I could punch. What would have happened to me if I hadn't taken him out with my first shot? I dread to think. The thing was the Old Bill had known what had gone on between us and still sent us to the same hospital. I could be lying in a mortuary now, and this cunt laying next to me, could have stabbed me, and cut me to pieces.

I end up going to Crown Court with the case, and at the time the police were taking road rage very very, serious, as it wasn't long after the Kenneth Noye road rage, murder case. I'd never been to court before and was the main witness in the case. He had a woman barrister who was about 4 ft tall defending him. I'd originally been charged with assault and Zorro the knifeman had been charged with A.B.H. When his brief started questioning me she got a bit stroppy.

"I'll put it to you Mr. Till that you went to my client's car, opened the door and punched him in the face."

I replied "I'll put it to you I never."

She turned around and faced the judge. She was clicking her heels and twiddling her thumbs behind her back and then dramatically turned quickly to face me.

"I'll put it to you once more Mr. Till that you did go to his car and that you did open his car door and that you did punch him in the face."

"I'll put it to you once again that I never," I replied.

She turned her back on me again and walked away, her thumbs going nine to the dozen in the base of her spine. She turned to face me.

"Mr. Till, I'll put it to you that you," and before she could finish I jumped in.

"I fucking told ya you cunt I never and don't listen to that fucking Elephant headed cunt." I shouted as I pointed across the courtroom at Zorro, who was sitting there, playing the innocent victim in all this.

The judge stopped the trial and slung me out of court and I was banged up in the cells for contempt of court. Before his brief had been questioning me I'd explained to the court that the man's injuries could have been a lot worse if it wasn't for the fact that I was a trained boxer and that I could control my emotions and deal with situations like these. It came through years of training as a professional fighter. I told the court that I knew how far I could go in restraining someone without them sustaining or suffering serious injury plus I wasn't a violent person outside the ring. If I'd have had steel toe capped boots on I could have kicked his head in and he would have never got up. What I had done was controlled, and I think the judge believed me, and then I'd gone and spoiled myself by rearing up and losing it, so my little speech went out the window. I'd fucked myself right up losing my rag. In the end the case was thrown out of court even though I had four witnesses, and one young fella even saw the bloke actually stab me. I didn't think I could lose but I did. I've never seen the bloke to this day. Perhaps he fucked off back to Kosovo, or where ever he came from. He's much safer there because if I ever bumped into him I'd finish the job he started.

I was out one night in Watford at the Kudos nightclub with a girl-friend and a few mates, and this bloke comes strolling over and asked if I was Andy Till the boxer. I smiled at him

"Yes mate I am," I said.

"Do you think you can still have a fight?" he asked me.

"Go away mate," I said "I'm not interested."

"No go on, do you think you can still have a fight?" and he stepped towards me.

"Look mate go away before you get hurt" I told him.

"Oh Yea" he said and half pushed me.

Crash! I caught him with a right hander and he was spark out before he hit the deck. The bouncers, who'd been watching the bloke, came over and picked him up and slung him out. His boxing career was over.

I've done a few different jobs since I quit boxing and also left the airport and I've done a bit of debt collecting. I never usually do a money job unless it's a 50/50, split what's owed down the middle. I never ask for the money, I just explain to who ever owes the debt what is expected of them and how much they owe the other party and usually the other people see common sense and pay up. I've never harmed or threatened anybody or demanded anything but I think they see my good looks and see sense, plus I have a very charming way about me. I think it's the way I come across and it's also very important to come across in the right manner. Being polite always helps and manners cost nothing.

I also got into a bit of acting. I had a part in the film 'The Face' where I played a villain just released from prison. I also joined an agency called 'The Uglies'. I never really got a lot of work from them, well I wouldn't, would I really because I'm a good-looking fella. But I had a part in Guy Ritchie's film, 'Snatch'. I got a thousand pounds, for that and the scene I was in was where I put a gun to my head and blew my brains out. It took an hour to film; not bad dough for an hour's work but I had to wait 3 months to get me money. It used to cost me 250 pounds a year to be registered with the agency so my acting career never paid the bills. I went to endless auditions and that costs money. You've got your fare on the trains and buses, you've got to eat while you're hanging about to be seen and the bottom end of the acting world is far from glamorous I can tell ya. My dream of Hollywood stardom didn't last long. But, I suppose like every job there is, some natural talent that slips through the net. Well that's the way I looked at it.

I've also now got an H.G.V. 2 driving licence so I used to do a bit of tipper driving for a mate of mine in one of his lorries. I've also worked for an agency doing a dust round. I had originally booked a block course of driving lessons with a learner school to get my H.G.V. licence but had run out of money when I'd spent £500, and then someone told me that I could get my licence if I signed on at the dole office, and then once I'd signed on the sausage roll I could sign on for one of the government driving courses. Anyway signing on was something I'd never done before. But I swallowed my pride and got my arse down there, I hated going in there, I really hated it. I just wanted to be able to go out and earn my own money. The bloke behind the desk, when I enquired about the driving course, told me I'd have to have been signing on for 6 months before they'd take me on for the H.G.V. course. I told him I didn't want to be a ponce and sign on, as it just wasn't me. I didn't like the idea of getting money for doing nothing. He looked at me puzzled.

"Have you got a criminal record?" he asked me.

I thought about lying, maybe giving the wrong answer, or even telling a white lie or bending the truth. I pondered on it for a second.

"Yes I have" I replied. Hanging my head in a kind of mock shame.

"Hang on a minute" he said, and wandered off into a back room. He wasn't gone long and came back to the desk smiling.

"Right Mr. Till you can start the driving course tomorrow."

"But hang on you've just told me that the minimum wait to get on the course was 6 months and now, because I'd admitted to having a criminal record, I'm being aloud to go straight on it." He smiled and nodded. It just showed crime does pay! The bloke started to fill out a few forms on the desk in front of me.

"I've only got an assault charge, but if I admit to a murder can you write me out an H.G.V. licence straight away?" I asked him.

He smiled wished me all the best shook my hand and handed me the completed paper work. He was true to his word and the next day I was on the course at Greenford. It took me three weeks to pass and in that time I was getting me dole money plus £17 a day traveling expenses. I passed the test at the second attempt me but I was well pleased I had another string to my bow. The criminal conviction I had acquired wasn't really down to me. I'd moved in with a bird and basically she fleeced me for a few quid. I'd decorated her place for her from top to bottom and I thought we were getting on well but behind my back she was shagging her brother's best mate. I came home one day and confronted her brother about it who promptly picked up a claw hammer and waved it in my face.

"Don't start nothing or you'll be getting this" he said, and with that he's cracked me over the head with it. I know as a boxer I couldn't use my fists as they're classed as lethal weapons so I grabbed him by the scruff of the neck and struck my head into his face about forty times. I cut his face to pieces. I didn't even know she was in the house and someone came up behind and hit me over the head with something. I turned around and stuck my nut on whoever it was that had just hit me, and it turned out to be her. The police were called and I ended up getting nicked and going to court and to cut a long story short I was found guilty. I told the judge they'd got their injuries not through me throwing punches but by me using my head to protect myself. I went through the whole rigmarole of explaining to the court that I wasn't allowed to hit anyone with my fists because of my boxing background. I knew that I was under oath so I wouldn't lie to the packed court. Would I? In the end I was given a £1,000 fine and 240 hours community service. Bearing in mind it was my first conviction I thought it was a bit harsh.

For my community service I had to go out and tidy up parks and pick up litter and wash down walls in local community centres around Hounslow and Uxbridge. I also worked inside a temple in Southall. We had to clean it up and give it a lick of paint. I had 20 hours left to do and I'd been working in this temple for nearly a week when one of the Indians who worked there asked me to take my shoes off when I came into the temple. I refused and he reported me to my probation officer. I was taken back to court and received another 40 hours community service. It was totally out of order. I don't take my shoes off to go in my own house. What's the old saying? "When in Rome do as the Romans do." It's one law for one and one law for another. I wouldn't be allowed to wear a dagger on the outside of my trousers but the people running the temple could. Before you call me a racist I'm not. I'm proud to be British and being proud of my country doesn't make me a racist. I did make one brief appearance back in the ring and that was when I was on holiday out in Tenerife. My brother in law had a bar over there and I got chatting to a fella in there while I was having a drink. The bloke heard from one of the regulars in there that I'd been a pro boxer. He told me he was the light heavyweight champion of Tenerife and that he would have liked to have had, a spar with me but I may be just a bit unfit and fat to get in the ring with him, "no disrespects Telly Tubby, but you might get hurt" he said.

"Don't worry about that" I told him and we carried on having a bit of light hearted banter, and, it was all in good fun. We were all mates together drinking and having a piss take. A couple of days later I met him down the local boxing gym and we got into the ring. I hadn't pulled a pair of gloves on for years. We got gloved up and without any head guards on off we went. He let a couple of shots go and fired off a couple of jabs into my guard, which I held, high. He moved around for a good minute and a half letting shots go. I just stood in the centre of the ring "is that all you've got mate, " I asked, "you've got to do better then that" and with that I moved towards him and sunk a hook deep into his ribs. He dropped to the canvas gasping for air " Come on" I said " you can't let a fat Telly Tubby do this to you" I could hear people at ringside laughing, quite a few people had come along to watch. He eventually got back up and we carried on sparring I caught him with a couple more shots and bloodied his nose. " Have you had enough of this fat Telly Tubby bashing you?" he nodded so that was that and we didn't see him in the bar for a few days. When he did turn up both his eyes were swollen and black and so was his ego. He bought me a drink, and shook my hand. " I'm not bad for an old fat man, am I? " He couldn't answer.

Nowadays I don't really follow boxing. There are too many manufactured and hyped fighters. I do go to the odd show and at times I'm called into the ring by the M.C. to take a bow but the buzz and the desire to fight have long gone. I'm happy now just being with my long time girlfriend, Carol, and her lovely family. Without her I dread to think where I'd be now. I still see my children who are now aged 20, 16 and 12, and I live with my nephew. I'm happy being a tipper driver and am more then happy and contented with my life. I know that in my boxing career I could and should have been a world champion, but then again, you can't turn back the pages of life. Seconds out!

GRAHAM STEVENS

I've known Andy for about 10 years and we met through people we both know, I'd done a bit of boxing and we sort of had a lot in common and we just sort of clicked. We met just as Andy's career was finishing; I lived not far from Andy, in Uxbridge, so I'd heard all about him. I was training to do some unlicensed fighting and bumped into him through our mutual friends, Joe Smith and Jimmy Stockins. I' m in the golf industry and run quite a big business in the golf trade. We are good mates now and at times get into bits of bother together. We've got into a few scrapes, but the thing is with Andy he'd fight any one if they were 2ft tall or 22ft tall it makes no odds to him.

When I was lined up for my first unlicensed bout he offered to help me train and it went really well, he pushed me hard, and put me through the same fitness programme he used as a pro. I sparred with a few different people who were sort of novices, then a few days before the fight Andy decided I needed to do a light 3 round spar with him, in the first round he came at me and hit me with some heavy body shots, and broke 3 of my ribs "it don't look like your up to it" he said as I was bent over double with the pain. He only done that, he said to prove to me that I wasn't up to getting in the ring. He says he wasn't being heavy handed, but I suspect he wanted to show who was boss. I was about 14 stone and he was about 19 stone, so there was a bit of weight difference. I was all right for about 30 seconds as I jabbed away and moved around with him, and I'm thinking this is ok, I'm not doing to bad and then he's gone and hit me with a couple of shots which backed me up onto the ropes, and then he's gone bang, bang right up the ribs. The wind was taken right out of me but I managed to get up. Joe Smith who was promoting the show wasn't best pleased about it. But Andy pleaded his innocence and told Joe he'd only given me a gentle tap. I ended up missing that show but fought on Joe's next one. I fought a great big fat X doorman who was trying to nut me and all sorts of things, he was 3 stone heavier then me and it was a right shit fight. He never really landed a clean shot on me and I never had a mark on me. He's since turned out to be a right, wrongen. I never had any more fights after that and the way I looked at it was that I didn't need to get myself a reputation. I didn't really need to do it, but it was something I wanted to try. I think a few years back if Andy had lost a bit of weight and got himself fit he would have made a great bare-knuckle or unlicensed fighter, he was made for it he was so strong and had that nasty streak you need to succeed. A few years back I bumped into boxing promoter Barry Hearn when I was flying out to Las Vegas, we got talking and I said you must know my mate Andy Till? "Funny enough" he said "I was only talking to someone about him only the other day and that is one bloke you wouldn't want to meet in a dark alley" I thought that was a nice compliment. To be truthful I could rely on Andy he's always been there when I've needed him and he's a good mate. The one thing when he's got no money and he lends a few bob off of me, he always makes sure he pays you back. To me that means a lot. I now run a golf company, which is one of the biggest in Europe and we turned over 15 million pounds last year. I'm also a pro golfer. Andy's done a few jobs for me and done a bit of debt collecting and is very good at his job and he seems to enjoy it.

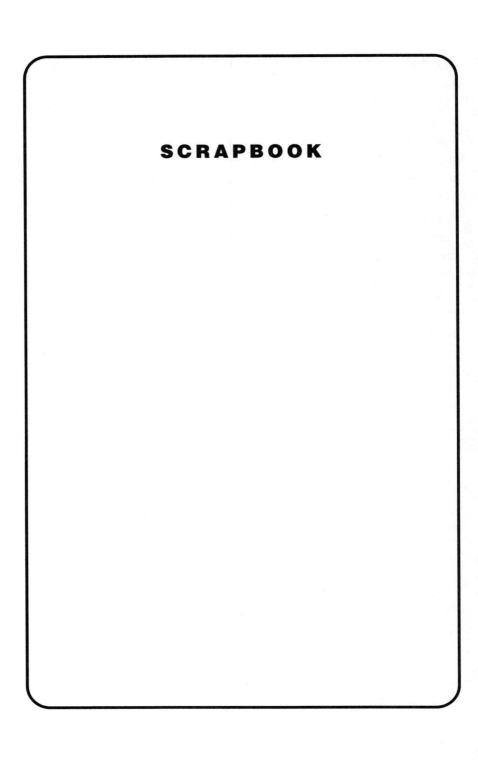

SCRAPBOOK

Friday 28th March is a big day in every boxers calender — The N.W. London Junior Championships are being held at Alexandra Palace's Palm Court and promise to be as exiciting as usual.

At just 16 years old Andrew Till is hot favourite to yet again get through to the final. Andy has been boxing for Northolt A.B.C. since the age of 12 and in that time has had 32 contests and won 25!

In 1979 he reached the semi-finals of the National Association of Boys' Clubs Championships and went on to win the National finals of the N.W. London Division and the London A.B.A. Unfortunately he was narrowly outpointed by young Christie of Coventry who rated the best Junior Boxer of that weight in Great Britain.

TILL DISASTER

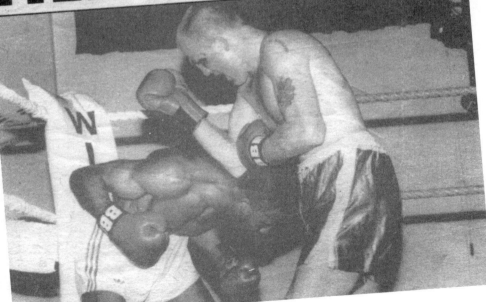

Till retains title after three round thriller

BEDFONT boxing king Harry Holland is celebrating after his top fighter Andy 'Stoneface' Till retained his British Light Welterweight title against Tony Collins last week.

Till, the fighting milkman from Northolt, won the title with a points verdict over Wally Swift after a memorable battle in September.

REPORT BY RAY CHUDLEY

He showed a lot of bottle to overpower Collins in his first defence, shown live on Sky Sports.

The fight was stopped in the third round - and a delighted Holland is now trying to set up a World Title bid.

"Andy has always been able to do it in the gym, but he's never quite put it together like that when it mattered," he told Chronicle Sport.

"I expected a full distance fight, similar to his battle with Swift. Even when he beat the champion he went to sleep for two or three rounds, but against Collins it was near perfection.

"His jab was sharp, his defence was terrific and his punching was full blooded.

"It's my job to find faults, but it's difficult. Gary Mason was very complimentary on the television - and rightly so.

"Collins just couldn't cope with Andy's strength and power."

Holland did not promote the fight at the York Hall, Bethnal Green, in order to concentrate on training his fighter. His next task is to secure a title shot for 'Stoneface'.

He revealed: "I am negotiating with representatives of David Jackson, the WBO champion, and Gianfranco Rosi, the IBF title holder.

"We don't mind travelling to Italy to face Rosi, though they say you have to knock them out to get a result over there.

"He is 34 now and is going to come apart at the seams sooner or later. Andy could be the one to do it."

If those options do not materialise, Till could make a voluntary defence or face number one challenger, Robert McCracken or Martin Smith, who meet in a forthcoming eliminator.

● *Champion Andy Till and Manager Harry Holland.*

Northolt boxer Andy Till wins British title

Champion!

NORTHOLT boxer and milkman Andy Till has been crowned British light middleweight champion

Andy, who boxed for Northolt ABC before turning professional, clinched a narrow points victory over title holder Wally Smith last Thursday.

In a bruising battle at Watford Town Hall, Till, now aged 29, beat Smith (who was defending his title for the third time) by just half a point after a dramatic finale.

His manager and promoter Harry Holland said: "It was a very close fight indeed. I had it about even until the last round but then Andy's strength clinched it.

"I'm convinced he won it in that last round and it was a fantastic performance. I would say it was one of the best fights seen in Britain this year."

The result was a tremendous boost for Till, who has spent the past couple of years building up to the fight.

It was always going to be a close affair, but the Northolt man had the edge psychologically after beating the champion three years ago in a non-title fight.

In front of a sell-out crowd, Swift had the best of the early exchanges but Till always took the fight to his opponent and relied on his strength to win a series of battling exchanges.

The Northolt man seemed to go to sleep around the sixth to eighth rounds but he came back with fiery punches in the latter stages, and clinched victory with an amazing display in the final round when he threw everything he had at a tiring Swift.

The capacity crowd rose to its feet at the end to cheer an incredible bout, and now both Till and Holland believe the road ahead is laden with gold.

Said Holland: "We've worked very hard to get Andy up to number one in Britain. Now we are chasing a world title. I can't promise anything, but that is what we are working on and aiming for.

"We need to get him up to number one in Europe, first. Last year he was ranked eight, but this win should push him up a bit."

If Till is made to wait for a European title fight, his first defence of his British title is likely to be as early as this December.

Harry said: "He's taking a well earned rest now. But we won't be hanging about. If he can't fight in Europe we will definitely have a voluntary defence before Christmas, and there is a big queue of fighters wanting a go."

Whatever happens, British champion Andy Till has done his manager, and Northolt, proud.

● *Northolt boxer Andy Till is held aloft after winning his British title at Watford*

TILL CASHES IN

Andy milks title glory

By MATT DRISCOLL

NORTHOLT milkman Andy Till delivered 12 rounds of stunning ferocity to snatch the British light middleweight crown from Wally Swift last night.

After a monumental battle in Watford Town Hall, Till completed the double over Nottingham's Swift and denied him a Lonsdale Belt.

The Daily Star sponsored fight promised to be a classic after their last encounter in 1989 which Till won on points.

And the night certainly lived up to expectations, with the two slugging it out toe-to-toe.

They rocked each other after just two rounds and looked capable of inflicting enough damage to send the fight either way.

Swift was marked around his left eye early on and Till soon had him on the ropes.

Then, after a venomous exchange, 26-year-old Swift suddenly stopped using his right hand.

He was forced to rely almost entirely on his left jab to score, and afterwards a ringside doctor revealed Swift had a suspected hairline fracture.

By the eighth a small cut had appeared below Swift's left eye as he desperately tried to claw back Till's lead.

But referee Mickey Vann finally gave it to Till 118-117½.

Swift insisted: "I damaged my right hand when I hit Till on the head in the third round. After that it was dead.

"But I'm certain I'll win back the title."

Till said: "This was the one I've been waiting for and everything went right. I knew I was capable of controlling it."

SWIFT SHOT: Till's forced to take evasive action Pic: LAWRENCE LUSTIG

Milko on the move

A MILKMAN joined more than 30,000 cyclists in a London to Brighton cycle ride for charity.

Andy Till 24, of Express Dairies, Yeading Lane, Northolt, was one of the thousands of people who got on their bikes last Sunday to raise money for the British Heart Foundation.

The cyclists were cheered off from Clapham Common on their 56 miles ride with crowds of people lining the way.

Andy said: "The crowds kept me going, whenever I felt like giving up they would egg me on. My cycling shorts helped too, the chamois leather stopped me getting a sore bum."

Andy is a professsinal boxer so he is used to having to keep fit and got into training before the ride by cyling 26 miles a day.

Although no one else from the dairy joined the ride, they all sponsored him and he raised more than £50.

Milkman Till radiates raw aggression of gladiator

BOXING   Steve Bunce

IF ANDY TILL and his cornermen swapped their modern tracksuits for ancient Roman attire and their gloves for *caestus* mitts they could easily pass for part of a wild mosaic.

When Till fights, the arena comes to life with a vitality that is absent in modern boxing and resembles the Coliseum the old. He has a loyal following of boxing-literate fans, not TV-educated spectators who drift in and out of the bigger promotions.

In September, Till won the British light-middleweight title after 18 gruelling fights and six years of arduous toil in the company of manager Harry Holland and coach Johnny Bloomfield. His ring history is written in scars and marks across his face.

Last Thursday night, with 500 fans roaring him on, Till climbed the steps once again to make his first defence. Bethnal Green's York Hall was sold out in anticipation of a battle. Put simply, Till gives value in a sport so badly devalued by confrontations made possible by the inadequacy of all ruling organisations and the power of television.

Till, 29, is not a television star . . . yet. So far, he has made only one brief appearance on BBC and two on a satellite channel. The awful truth, in a brutal game increasingly dominated by bewildering amounts of money, is that terrestrial television demands far less of its chosen few than Till is prepared to give.

His fights would literally dumbfound a viewing public who have become increasingly numbed by Chris Eubank's outrages and Frank Bruno's inane chat.

In the far corner on Thursday evening was former "child" star Tony Collins, who had fought most of his 29 fights in front of television cameras. Despite an early career consisting of quick wins against well-paid television extras, Collins developed into a real prospect. Young, good-looking and with a solid punch in either hand, he has become a real fighter.

Meanwhile, away from the cameras, Till honed his raw skills in small halls in even fights. Hard encounters against hard men, until a break in 1990 matched him against Manchester's Ensley Bingham in a final eliminator for the British title.

In the packed arena, Till became increasingly frustrated and eventually — like a throwback to the gladiator he resembles — he repeatedly smashed his elbow into the back of Bingham's head. Bad blood was contained to the ring and Till, who acts like a perfect gentleman outside it, regrets the incident and has fought a clean fight since.

Bingham challenged for the title but was knocked out by Wally Swift. Till had earlier beaten Swift in a breathtaking fight that extended the limits of bravery and skill and led to £58 in "nobbins" being tossed on to the blood-speckled canvas in appreciation of the endeavours of both men.

Swift defended against Collins in a lively 12-round encounter and finally met Till at Watford Town Hall in September. The cameras arrived for a live broadcast and a new warrior champion was born after 12 rounds of solid effort.

When Till's robe came off on Thursday night, his tattooed arms, heavy shoulders and shaven skull clashed with the slim body of ponytailed Collins. Despite the physical differences, few were prepared for what happened next.

From the opening bell to the fight being stopped in less than three rounds, Till unleashed a level of controlled brutality rarely seen in the British ring these days. Three times Collins stumbled and fell from an assortment of mighty blows and three times he courageously climbed to his feet again.

Till's grimace remained set in stone until the referee raised his hand as a weary Collins was led back to his corner, beaten but standing.

Till went home to resume his secure job as a milkman. There is talk of a world title fight in March, but boxing talk is usually hopeful, often fanciful and seldom so'id.

However, a confer ice has been called for Tuesday when we might hear something about the Middlesex milkman's next round.

Till is tops

by FRANK WARD

ANDY TILL'S ferocious fourth-round assault bludgeoned Wally Swift to defeat as he retained his British light-middleweight title at the Royal Albert Hall last night.

Middlesex powerhouse Till was too strong and persistent for the challenger, who failed to go the distance for the first time in 36 fights.

Referee Larry O'Connell called a halt after 24 seconds of the round following a wicked Till left hook which had Swift sagging on the ropes. The former champion protested that he was fit to continue — but he had already taken a beating and was cut over the right eye.

O'Connell was probably justified to err on the side of caution.

Till said: "I thought I had him in the second round, but the referee was right to step in, otherwise Wally could have been really hurt.?

Till blows big gamble

ANDY TILL lost a £56,000 gamble last night when he was retired at the end of four punishing rounds against European light-middleweight boxing champion Laurent Boudouani at Picketts Lock, North London, writes JOHN LLOYD.

Till's manager, Harry Holland, said: "Andy had a bad cut over the right eye and I had no option.

"It took £56,000 of Frank Maloney's and my money to get the Frenchman to London and we knew we were up against a dangerous opponent."

Till, from Northolt, took mandatory counts of eight in the second and third rounds and needed 17 stitches in face wounds.

TILL CASHES IN

MILKMAN Andy Till has got the bottle for a world title shot.

by STEVE READY

And manager Harry Holland is pushing for a tilt at either the WBO or WBA crowns.

Till put himself in contention by defeating Wally Swift to take the British light middleweight title earlier this week.

. And now he is keen to meet either WBO holder John David Jackson or WBA top man Vinny Pazienza.

"We will go anywhere for a world title fight because it is now or never for Andy, "said Holland.

"I have had talks with Jackson and Pazienza and I am hoping to secure Andy a big money fight in America early next year.

"Andy is dedicated and deserves his crack at a world title."

Till staged a last round rally against Swift that tipped the balance his way.

Swift injured his right hand in the third round but refused to use it as an excuse for a narrow points defeat.

He said: "I cannot take anything away from Andy because he boxed a very hard fight and was given the closest of decisions."

Till said: "Wally was terrific, I will give him that — but I won this war just like I won our first war three years ago."

◆ ANDY TILL

CUT DOWN

ANDY TILL was brutally beaten into submission after four rounds in his vain bid to lift the European light-middleweight title last night.

By IAN GIBB

The British champion had to be retired by his corner, badly gashed around both eyes. He had been floored twice and outclassed by Laurent Boudouani at Picketts Lock, North London.

The 27-year-old Frenchman was vicious as well as being too smart and powerful for the Northolt man.

Till nicknamed "Stoneface" because of his tough fighting style, found it was not nearly enough against the champion, who wasn't afraid to use his head when the Londoner tried to mix it inside.

Boudouani found Till's face right from the start and easily took the first round. Then he caught Till with a left in the second and sent him sprawling to the canvas with a short right.

Till was up at three and took the mandatory eight count before roaring back with blind courage.

A left hook bowled him over again in the third. He was up at three, but in bad trouble and his left eye was badly cut.

In the fourth the ex-milkman hurled himself at the champion, only to reel away with a badly cut right eye. The blood poured out of it as Boudouani hammered away.

Till appealed to the referee, but Dutch official Heink Mejers had little sympathy as the challenger had been using his own head.

Till was a bloody mess as the bell ended the fourth and his corner had no option but to call it off.

It was also a bad night for former British and European welterweight champion Kirkland Laing.

He was halted by cuts in the fifth round against Kevin Leushing for the vacant Southern Area Light middleweight title.

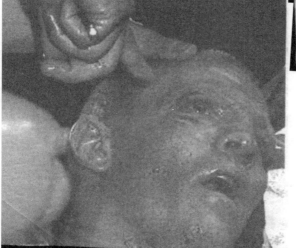

Frank Maloney & Harry Holland In Association With Panix Entertainment

Proudly Present

SPONSORED BY **SPX**
SPONSORED BY **SPX**

THE PEOPLE'S HEROES

12x3 min rounds
For The LIGHT MIDDLEWEIGHT CHAMPIONSHIP
OF EUROPE

LAURENT BOUDOUANI   ANDY TILL

V

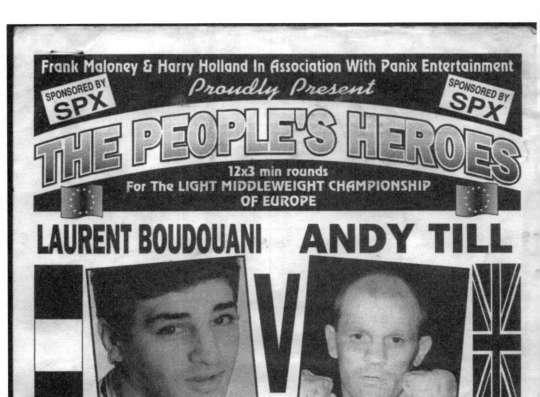

CHAMPION - FRANCE

CHALLENGER - NORTHHOLT
BRITISH & WBC INTERNATIONAL CHAMPION

10x3 min Rounds of Boxing for the Light Middleweight Championship of The Southern Area Between

KEVIN LEUSHING
'The Look'
BECKENHAM

V

KIRKLAND LAING
HACKNEY

10x3 min Rounds of Boxing for the Lightweight Championship of The Southern Area Between

ROCKY MILTON
CYPRUS CYCLONE

V

FELIX KELLY
HAMMERSMITH

10x3 min Rounds of Boxing for Championship of The Southern Area

ALI FORBES v RICHARD BUSTIN
SYDENHAM   NORWICH

8x3 min Rounds Super Middleweight Contest Between

IAN STRUDWICK v HUSSAIN SHAH
BECKENHAM   HOUNSLOW

ALSO FEATURING FUTURE STARS

ADRIAN DODSON • ROBERT ALLEN • JOEL ANI • CARLOS CHASE
ISLINGTON   U.S.A.   TOTTENHAM   WATFORD

WED 23rd JUNE 1993

PICKETTS LOCK CENTRE
EDMONTON

Lee Valley *Leisure* Park

Doors Open 7.00pm Boxing Commences at 8.00pm

Tickets: £50 £40 £30 £20
AVAILABLE FROM:

Champion Enterprises	071-249 9400
Harry Holland	081-890 4030
Kevin Leushing	081-336 5772
Thomas 'A' Becket	071-703 7334
Dennis Lewis	0860 924107
Brian Lynch	0708 250291 - 0708 223432
Ring Blackfriars	071-926 2589

R&B Printers, Eastbourne (0323)733378

LIGHT-MIDDLEWEIGHT

British champion: ANDY TILL

1 - Andy Till (Northolt)
2 - Lloyd Honeyghan (Bermondsey)
    (Commonwealth champion)
3 - Robert McCracken (Birmingham)
4 - Wally Swift (Birmingham)
5 - Martin Smith (Sheffield)
6 - Ensley Bingham (Manchester)
7 - Paul Wesley (Birmingham)
8 - Steve Foster (Manchester)
9 - Tony Collins (Yateley)
10 - Richard Okumu (Tottenham)
11 - Damien Denny (Belfast)
12 - Warren Stowe (Burnley)
     (Central Area champion)
13 - Carlos Colarusso (Llanelli)
     (Welsh champion)
14 - Kevin Sheeran (Crawley)

---

15 - Derek Wormald (Rochdale)
16 - Clay O'Shea (Islington)
17 - Jamie Robinson (West Ham)
18 - John Bosco (Bermondsey)
19 - Dean Cooper (Bristol)
     (Western Area champion)
20 - Gary Osborne (Walsall)
21 - Mark Jay (Newcastle)
22 - Paul Lynch (Swansea)
23 - Newton Barnett (Camberwell)
24 - Mark Cichocki (Hartlepool)
     (Northern Area champion)
25 - Horace Fleary (Huddersfield)
26 - Ian Chantler (St. Helens)
27 - Lee Ferrie (Coventry)
28 - Kevin Adamson (Walthamstow)
29 - Tony Velinor (Stratford)
30 - Robin Reid (Warrington)
31 - Adrian Dodson (St. Pancras)
32 - Winston May (West Ham)

Tim Carter
16 Newton Road
Burton-on-Trent
Staffs

Dear Mr. Till,

I have always found you an exciting fighter to watch, you're all action and it was a sad loss when you announced your retirement.

I looked forward to your comeback against Darron Griffiths and I was disgusted by the referees actions to stop the fight as youve been in worst trouble than that and have come back to win. Im sure you would have worn him down and stopped him in about the 7th. I hope you will fight on. Would it be possible to please send me a signed photo of yourself please as your one of my favourite fighters and youll be champion again.

All the best,
Your fan,

ANDY TILL

FORMER UNDEFEATED SOUTHERN AREA LIGHT-MIDDLEWEIGHT CHAMPION.
FORMER UNDEFEATED WBC INTERNATIONAL LIGHT-MIDDLEWEIGHT CHAMPION.

THE LIGHT-MIDDLEWEIGHT CHAMPION OF GREAT BRITAIN.

PROFESSIONAL RECORD

Date	Opponent	Result		Rounds	Venue
01.09.86	Peter Reid	W	TKO	6	Ealing.
25.09.86	Graham Jenner	W	PTS	6	Crystal Palace.
10.11.86	Randy Henderson	W	PTS	6	Longford
11.01.87	Tony Lawrence	W	TKO	4	Ealing
18.02.87	Ian Bayliss	W	PTS	6	Fulham
30.04.87	Dean Scarfe	L	PTS	8	Battersea
14.09.87	Andy Wright	W	TKO	2	Crystal Palace.
19.02.88	Geoff Sharpe	W	TKO	5	Longford
29.11.88	W.O. Wilson	W	PTS	10	Battersea

(Eliminator for the Southern Area Lt-Middleweight Championship)

Date	Opponent	Result		Rounds	Venue
01.03.89	WALLY SWIFT	W	PTS	8	Bethnal Green
12.06.89	Tony Britton	W	RTD	8	Battersea

(Vacant Southern Area Light-Middleweight Championship)

Date	Opponent	Result		Rounds	Venue
10.11.89	Nigel Fairbairn	W	TKO	8	Battersea
14.03.90	Steve Foster	W	RTD	5	Battersea
06.06.90	Ensley Bingham	L	DIS	3	Battersea

(Final Eliminator, British Light-Middleweight Championship)

Date	Opponent	Result		Rounds	Venue
12.09.90	Alan Richards	W	PTS	8	Battersea
06.02.91	Alan Richards	W	PTS	8	Battersea
01.06.91	Terry Magee	W	TKO	4	Bethnal Green
15.10.91	John Davies	W	PTS	12	Dudley

(Vacant WBC International Light-Middleweight Championship)

Date	Opponent	Result		Rounds	Venue
17.09.92	WALLY SWIFT	W	PTS	12	Watford

(British Light-Middleweight Title Challenge)

Date	Opponent	Result		Rounds	Venue
10.12.92	Tony Collins	W	TKO	3	Bethnal Green

(Defence of British Light-Middleweight Championship)

Date	Opponent	Result		Rounds	Venue
14.04.93	Wally Swift	W	TKO	4	Kensington

(Defence of British Light-Middleweight Championship)

SUMMARY>   Fights: 21   Won: 19   Lost: 2   Stoppages: 10